Hometown Investment Trust Funds

Naoyuki Yoshino · Sahoko Kaji
Editors

Hometown Investment Trust Funds

A Stable Way to Supply Risk Capital

Springer

Editors
Naoyuki Yoshino
Professor of Economics
Keio University
2-15-45 Mita, Minato-ku
Tokyo 108-8345
Japan

Sahoko Kaji
Professor of Economics
Keio University
2-15-45 Mita, Minato-ku
Tokyo 108-8345
Japan

ISBN 978-4-431-54753-2 ISBN 978-4-431-54309-1 (eBook)
DOI 10.1007/978-4-431-54309-1
Springer Tokyo Heidelberg New York Dordrecht London

Printed on acid-free paper

Springer is part of Springer Science+Business Media (www.springer.com)

Preface

In the early 1990s, Japan's real estate and stock market bubble burst and the economy went into a tailspin. The blame was put on Japan's unique financial intermediation, which was called the "collateral principle" because it allowed lending regardless of the viability of the project as long as there was collateral. Adopting Anglo-American ways of finance subsequently became a national goal in Japan.

Twenty years later, the Lehman crisis nearly tipped the entire world economy into an abyss. Anglo-American ways of finance were discredited. To the Japanese, there was no longer a model that ensured success and stability. At around the same time, a catastrophic earthquake and tsunami struck north-eastern Japan. During the long and painful recovery process an acute need for financing local SMEs and start-up companies came to light, and there was a simultaneous groundswell of desire among the Japanese people to help in and contribute to the recovery process. Many of these potential providers of capital were looking not for high returns but simply for an opportunity to do their own small share. Obviously, we needed a meeting place for these borrowers and lenders. In addition, Japan's government budget deficit to GDP ratio breeched 200 %, and the efficiency and effectiveness of public investment came into doubt. Private financing with transparent performance was called for.

This book explains the new form of financial intermediation that thus emerged and became one of Japan's national strategies. The new form of financial intermediation is called the "Hometown Investment Trust" fund or HIT, reflecting its goal to connect fund providers and their hometowns. One of its earliest proponents was Naoyuki Yoshino, co-editor and author of the first chapter explaining its background. Once the idea of HIT was launched, a committee was formed at the Cabinet Office to study it. As it quickly became clear, the HIT concept blended in perfectly with two ongoing efforts. One was the post-Lehman effort by the private and public sectors in the area of real estate and infrastructure investment funds. In Chap. 2, Atsuo Akai explains HIT in relation to Japan's real estate and infrastructure investment funds and schematises the overall picture of the emerging financial intermediation. The other of these ongoing efforts was the activities of a certain Japanese company established in 2000, Music Securities, which all started with one young drummer's desire to raise funds for his fellow musicians. This young drummer, Masami Komatsu, is now CEO of the company and explains their operations in Chap. 3. Chapter 4, written by Norifumi Sugimoto, provides two concrete examples to elaborate how HIT contributes to post-disaster reconstruction. In Chap. 5, written by Yuka Morita, we turn our eyes to Asia and Music Securities' activities towards poverty reduction. Shuhei Shiozawa concludes the book in Chap. 6 with a summary and some thoughts on prospects for the future.

As will become clear in the following chapters, the new method of financial intermediation has three main advantages.

Firstly, it contributes to financial market stability by lowering information asymmetry and distributing risk. The pre-Lehman "originate and distribute" model ended in disaster, because the borrowers' IOUs were submerged and dispersed deep inside complicated financial instruments. Once markets lost faith in the ability of borrowers to pay back, nobody knew where the risks were. Everyone became suspicious of each other and credit markets froze. It was completely false to assume that "distributing" risk in this manner contributed to stability. Information ended up being as asymmetric as it could possibly be. In contrast, the new method of financial intermediation presented in this book contributes to stability because it *lowers* information asymmetry. Individual households (and firms, if they want to invest in other companies) are keen to obtain information on the borrowing firms, mainly SMEs. The lenders are from the same "hometown" as, or share a hobby or taste with, the borrowers in which they take a personal interest. In addition, there is the low degree of both scale and concentration; both lenders and borrowers are relatively small and dispersed. Thus this financial intermediation distributes risk but not in a way that renders them invisible.

The second advantage of HIT is that it becomes a new source of much needed risk-capital. Financial regulations, notably the BIS capital adequacy ratio, are being tightened because banks and other financial institutions are now recognised as a potential source of instability. This may contribute to lowering risk in a macroprudential sense but is detrimental to the supply of risk capital. The situation is especially serious for firms with low or no collateral. In this environment, this new type of financial intermediation can be a new, important and stable source of risk capital.

The third advantage of HIT is that it is project-driven. First there is the pool of projects, from which investors choose to invest in. This is what makes this different from arrangements such as the Grameen Bank, which start with a fund whose destinations are chosen later. Investors are not necessarily seeking high returns. Rather, they are eager to help a project that they feel strongly about, because the project is in their hometown, reduces poverty, contributes to recovery from disaster, or satisfies their environmental concerns. For investors, this gives the added satisfaction of actually being able to "see" the thankful and smiling faces of the borrowers. In contrast, investors cannot see where their money goes when investing in ordinary mutual funds.

This will be a simultaneous publication in Japanese and in English. We aim to encourage policymakers, economists, lenders and borrowers from around the world (especially in developing countries) to adopt this new form of financial intermediation. HIT provides an alternative to existing direct and indirect financial intermediation, both of which have proven to be prone to instability if not disaster.

It cannot be foreseen at this stage what percentage of financial intermediation will shift to this new method. In the event that HIT becomes at least as dominant as the more traditional ways of intermediation, it has the potential to increase employment, at the SMEs as well as in the pool of retirees from financial institutions. If the SMEs can borrow, they can hire. But in order for a system such as HIT to work well, the intermediaries between the borrowers and lenders must be experienced in the trade of financial intermediation. There will subsequently be a high demand for people who have retired from (larger) financial institutions after pursuing successful careers.

It is our sincere hope that this volume will contribute to the increased recognition and use of this new method and ultimately to global financial stability.

The papers included in this volume were presented and discussed at a conference held in Tokyo at the end of September 2012. The financial support of Nomura Securities for the conference as well as the publication is gratefully acknowledged.

Tokyo, Japan

Naoyuki Yoshino
Sahoko Kaji

Contents

Chapter 1
The Background of Hometown Investment Trust Funds

Naoyuki Yoshino

1 Overview

This chapter will, first of all, describe how the flow of funds in Japan functions. Second, it explains how Hometown Investment Trust (HIT) funds can fund businesses that are likely to grow in future and are capable of making a social contribution, but entail risks. HIT funds have recently begun to grow, and we will make the case for the urgent need to foster such funds. There are two main reasons why this is important. First, as BIS capital adequacy requirements become more stringent worldwide, banks find it more difficult to provide funding to high-risk businesses and projects. Second, Japan's public finances are in dire straits. Local businesses outside the main urban centres used to be supported by subsidies from the centre to local regions in the form of national tax revenues allocated to local governments, national treasury disbursements, and government loan and investment funds. Under today's expanding fiscal deficits, however, issuance of deficit-financing bonds to provide for local regions has reached a limit (see Fig. 1.1), and the need to use private-sector funds to finance regional projects has become urgent (Yoshino and Mizoguchi 2013; McNelis and Yoshino 2012).

The second half of this chapter will describe the flow of funds in Asia. Chapter 5 of this book will discuss concrete examples in Asia, where the financial systems also rely heavily on indirect financing via banks, so that the supply of funds to risk sectors is very likely to taper off. It is necessary to create mechanisms to supply various kinds of funds, including HIT funds that finance new corporations, businesses and environmental programs.

N. Yoshino (✉)
Keio University, Tokyo, Japan
e-mail: yoshino@econ.keio.ac.jp

N. Yoshino and S. Kaji (eds.), *Hometown Investment Trust Funds: A Stable Way to Supply Risk Capital*, DOI 10.1007/978-4-431-54309-1_1, © Springer Japan 2013

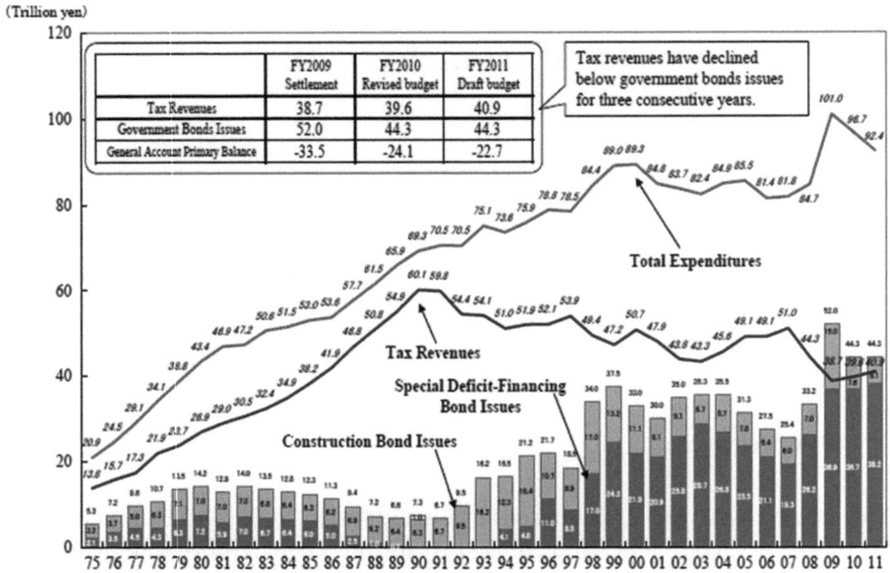

Fig. 1.1 General account expenditures, tax revenues and government bond issues

2 The Flow of Funds in Japan

2.1 Differences in Asset Management in Japan and the West

Figure 1.2 shows how private individuals in different countries distribute their funds. Left is the United States, in the middle is Japan, and right is Germany. The size of each pie chart shows the total amount of personal-sector financial assets under management. The personal-sector financial assets in the United States amount to 3,758 trillion yen, which is twice or more the figure for Japan.

It is a characteristic of the United States that cash and savings amount to about 15% of total financial assets. In Japan, cash and savings are nearly 60% of assets managed, followed by pension funds and insurance. The amount of marketable securities and shares is extremely small. The downward trend in share prices due to the economic slump is likely to reduce this amount yet further. If that were to happen, then the question of who would provide the money for corporations, environmental projects, and so on in regions with possibilities for growth but which carry risk becomes extremely problematical. If not handled properly, the flow of funds through Japan's financial institutions could end up going only to borrowers that are safe, and corporations with possibilities for growth could be nipped in the bud.

In the United States and England, by contrast, the environment for risk-taking is in place. In the United States, half or more of assets are in share and marketable securities. Private individuals are therefore powerfully motivated to take risks with

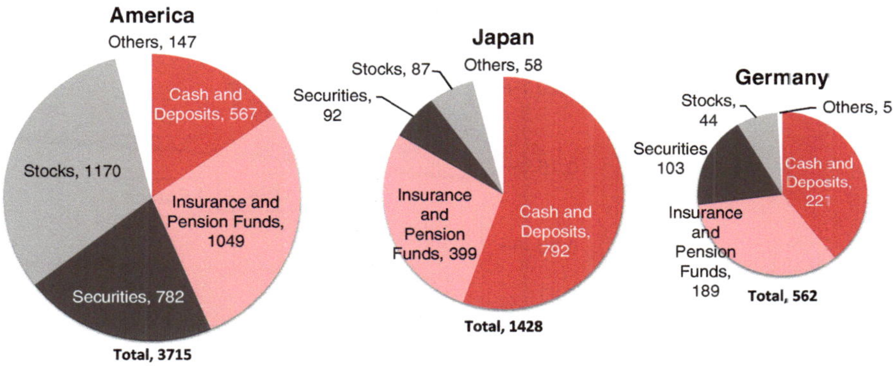

Fig. 1.2 Financial asset allocation of US, Japan and Germany

high returns in mind. Germany used to resemble Japan in this regard. As it happened, however, the emergence of investment trusts and the sell-off of shares for privatization yielded profits for large numbers of people, and the movement of assets into shares and investments has accelerated (Yoshino and Mizoguchi 2013).

In the case of shares from privatization in Japan, Nippon Telegraph and Telephone Corporation (NTT) and Japan Tobacco, Inc. (JT), shares were sold, but their prices then declined. Ultimately, private individuals could not channel their investments into equities.

Figure 1.3 shows comparisons of income from interest and dividends divided by income, by country. Japan is at the very bottom, and the Japanese people clearly are not living off income from interest and dividends. In Germany, on the other hand, the economy is doing well and the performance of investments and equities is good, putting their interest and dividends income as a percentage of total income at the very top.

Judging from Fig. 1.3, the Japanese are engaging in investment, but the fact is that their earnings as a percentage of income are the lowest in the OECD. Two points to grasp from this are, first, that something needs to be done to raise investment returns, and second, that somehow investment needs to be channelled into highly profitable projects and businesses.

2.2 *The Mechanism of the Flow of Funds*

Figure 1.4 shows what the flow of funds in Asia as a whole looks like, and how it differs from the flow of funds in the United States and Europe. In the middle, we see policy finance, long-term credit banks, banks, and SME-oriented financial institutions. These are ordinary banks, and the financial structure of Asia, as shown in Fig. 1.4, is bank-centred (dependent mainly on indirect financing). The bond market, shown at the very top, has hardly developed at all, except for the market for

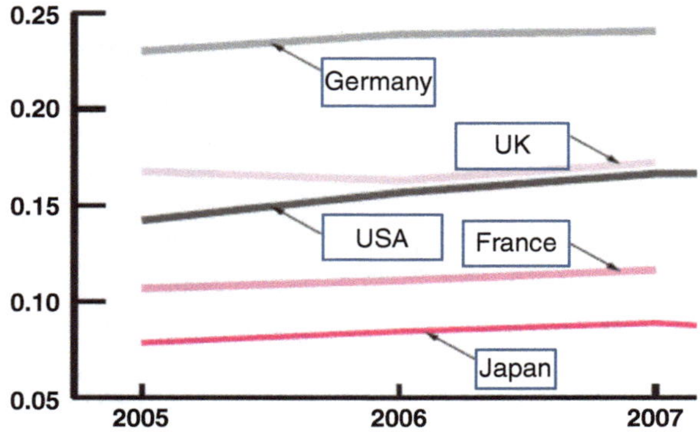

Fig. 1.3 Revenue share of financial assets Germany, UK, USA, France and Japan

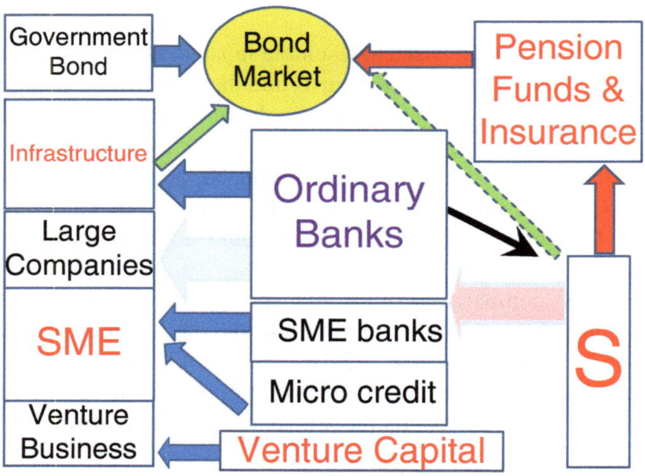

Fig. 1.4 Mechanism of the flow of funds in Asia. *S* savings

government bonds. Venture capital, shown at the very bottom, likewise hardly exists. The non-bank known as micro credit, shown second from the bottom in the figure, does exist in Asia (Yoshino 2012).

Under these circumstances, one wonders who will provide funds for venture businesses, shown at the bottom left of Fig. 1.4, and other such new enterprises. And, who will provide risk capital to the local enterprises, second from the bottom, that entail risks, or to the SMEs that also present risk? There is an urgent need to build the mechanisms to do these things. This is because, even though SME-oriented financial institutions do exist, they are banks and therefore face increasing difficulty in providing risk capital due to the increasing stringency of Basel capital adequacy requirements, which will be explained at a later point. In terms of large projects, this is illustrated by the fact that private-sector funding is rarely channelled into infrastructure improvement and other such activities, such as seen near the top left of the figure. This is a distinctive characteristic of Japan and Asia. It is an urgent task, therefore, to provide Japan and other Asian countries, where there is no venture capital merely local non-bank (micro credit), with new investment funds such as HIT funds, the topic of this work, so that money will flow to local small enterprises (venture business) and local SMEs.

Another crucial matter is that providers of long-term funding must be fostered. The pension funds and insurance at the upper right of the figure are institutional investors that engage in long-term investments. It seems likely that pension funds and life insurance companies will undergo considerable development in Asia in the future. Other Asian countries are starting to catch up to Japan in becoming aging societies. The problem in Japan is that the funds amassed in pension funds and by insurance companies are being invested almost entirely in government bonds so that, unfortunately, they do not reach the private sector.

In the United States and England, by contrast, pension funds and insurance companies act as institutional investors and place their money in infrastructure improvement and other long-term projects. What needs to be considered in Japan is how to manage the assets that have been accumulated as long-term funds by pension funds and insurance companies. In other parts of Asia, pension funds and insurance companies will also be developing as economies grow and populations age. The manner in which they make investments as long-term asset managers is of great importance in terms of the flow of funds in their economies.

2.3 Effects of Declining Personal Savings Rates and Aging of the Population

Figure 1.5 shows household savings rates in several countries. The rise visible in 1998 is in South Korea. The reason for this sharp increase is that income, which is the denominator of the personal savings rate (savings/income) dropped sharply due to the Asian currency crisis of 1997–1998, making the personal savings rate appear to be higher. Looking at Japan, it is apparent that the household savings rate has been rapidly and steadily declining. In the context of a declining personal savings rate, the question of how to increase funds for local communities and for hometowns is a key issue in terms of the flow of funds in Japan as a whole. Up to now, the central government provided funds to local regions outside the main urban centres in the form of national tax revenues allocated to local governments and national treasury disbursements. As fiscal deficits increase, however, private-sector funds will have to be directed to local corporations and local projects or the funds for investment in hometowns will dwindle away.

The declining personal savings rate in Japan is a result of three main factors: (1) incomes are growing at a low rate; (2) the population growth rate is low, which means the number of children has been diminishing; and (3) the pension and social security systems in Japan have reached a certain degree of maturity.

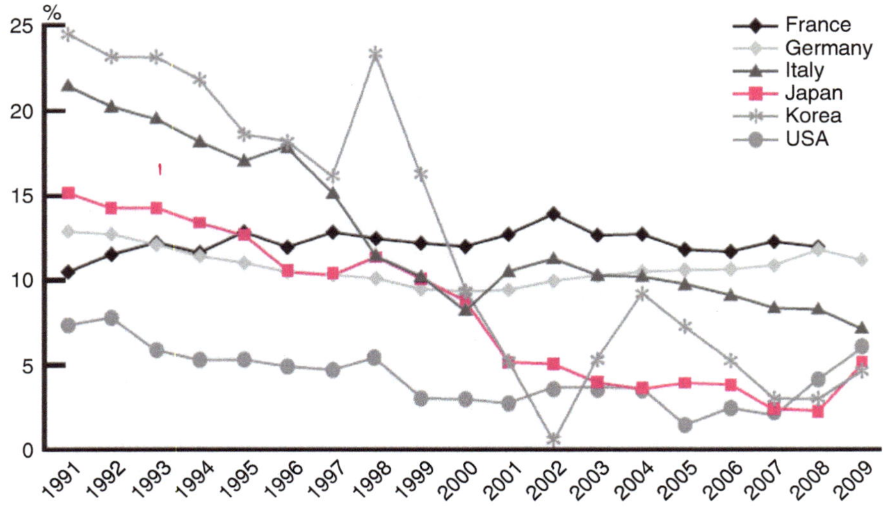

Fig. 1.5 Households' savings rate Korea, Italy, Japan, Germany, France and USA

In China, however, the situation is reversed: (1) incomes are growing at a rapid rate; (2) the population is also still growing; and (3) old-age social security is not developed. Consequently, the personal savings rate in China is rising.

Figure 1.6 shows the aging of the population in Japan. If matters continue as they are, the number of elderly people will continue to increase whilst the number of people of working age in the middle will grow smaller. As things are, the personal savings rate will decline, social security and pensions for the elderly will run short, and the funds that can be directed to local and hometown investment will disappear.

2.4 *Basel Capital Adequacy Requirements and Their Effects*

The discussion will now turn to the effects of the Basel capital adequacy requirements (Revankar and Yoshino 2008). The banking sector is presently subject to capital adequacy ratio criteria. On the right of the figure under the bank's liabilities side are the bank assets (liquidity), indicating the amount of net assets the bank is obligated to hold against the risk of the loans made by the bank. Furthermore, not only must banks retain assets against the risk of loans made, but since *the Lehman crisis*, banks are being required to set aside a certain amount of capital against liquidity risk. The purpose of enhancing capital adequacy is to address a possible increase in non-performing loans shown on the asset side to the left in the figure. If such an increase were to occur, and those bad loans could be covered with the bank's own capital, then there would be no burden on depositors. This is why capital adequacy requirements made their appearance. In the example in Fig. 1.7, this

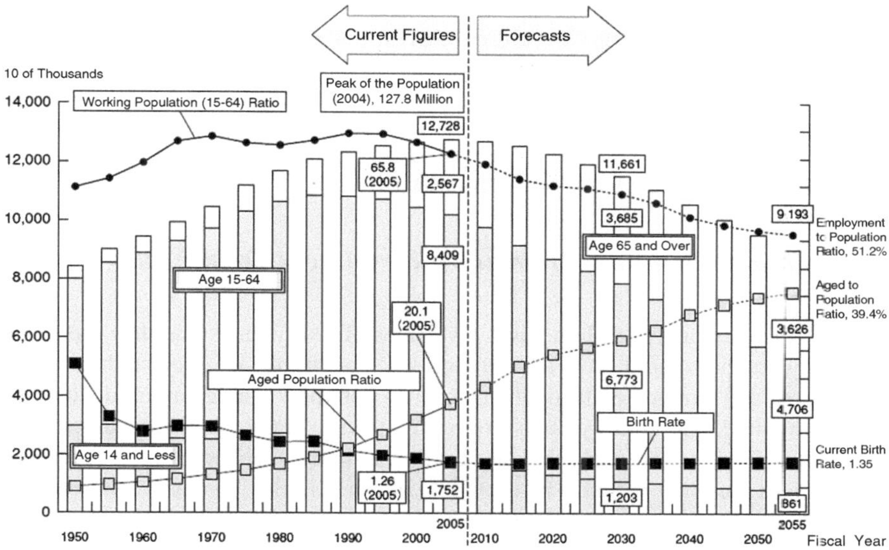

Fig. 1.6 Population structure of Japan

Fig. 1.7 Basel capital requirement

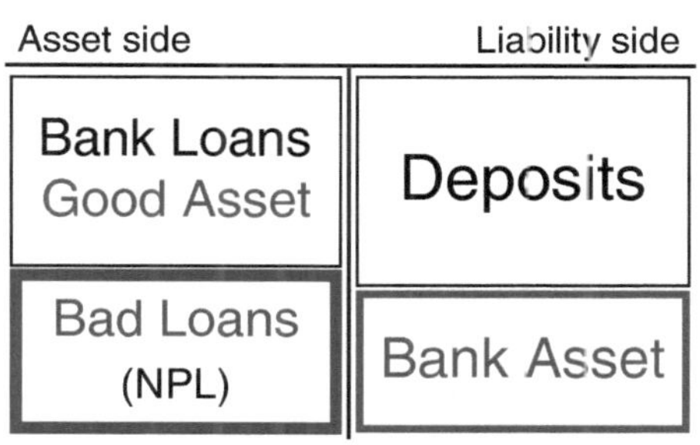

bank's assets are smaller than its bad loans which means it is insolvent and may collapse. In order to prevent this happening, the bank must set aside assets in an amount equal to or exceeding its non-performing loans. In simple terms, this is the significance of the Basel capital adequacy requirements (Yoshino and Hirano 2011).

Consequently, as risks increase, it is required that a larger amount of a bank's assets in Fig. 1.7 have to be set aside, and funds directed into assets that are safer. Furthermore, if the Basel requirements for capital adequacy ratio grow more stringent, then it is to be expected that banks will find it extremely difficult, in the future, to lend money to local businesses that are subject to risk. Similarly, it will no doubt become more difficult to lend out the money amassed from deposits to small enterprises and enterprises that entail risks. That is because, if a bank were to decide to provide funds to small businesses or to SMEs bearing risk, then that bank would have to set aside more of its own capital. So long as the kind of Hometown Investment Trust funds proposed in this work do not exist, the flow of funds to venture businesses, small enterprises, and local small enterprises will tend to dry up.

3 Hometown Investment Trust Funds

3.1 Characteristics of Hometown Investment Trust Funds

One distinctive feature of Hometown Investment Trust funds is that they are funds that know the borrower's face. An ordinary investment trust is set up so that money is gathered and handled collectively and we do not know where any particular part of it is invested, but it does yield a return (dividends). In the case of the investment funds described in this work, they are funds that know their borrowers' faces and that support the local region. The provision of funds in this way is investment that can contribute to the region. In that sense, it also becomes possible to create a fund that combines donation and investment.

The following chapters will describe the Hometown Investment Trust funds using various examples.

3.2 Providing Development Funds to Local Regions

Up to now, banks have engaged in loans to local borrowers, including enterprises that bear a certain degree of risk. In future, however, they will be less able to take risks with money put together from deposits. This is because Basel capital adequacy requirements set by the Bank for International Settlements (BIS) discussed above are becoming more stringent. It is necessary that money be collected in the form of HIT funds that are able to complement the activities carried out so far by banks, and that these funds be directed to enterprises that show promise of future growth even though they entail risk, such as solar power generation and other such projects that can improve the environment and contribute to local communities.

Figure 1.8 shows a macro view of stock price movements in Japan. If the Japanese economy gradually shrinks, then it naturally follows that average stock prices will go down. If this is the case, then even investments made according to macro averages will never show any increase in productivity (return) so long as we do not seek out good projects and invest in those that appear likely to grow. Japan is a country with little economic growth, and stock price movements will also go stagnant. In a stagnant economy, it is also necessary to make separate investments in funds and projects that show growth potential, to borrowers who we see as individuals. In other words, hand-made investments are required. The reason is that profitability (meaning returns) will not increase if our focus is on average investment as a whole.

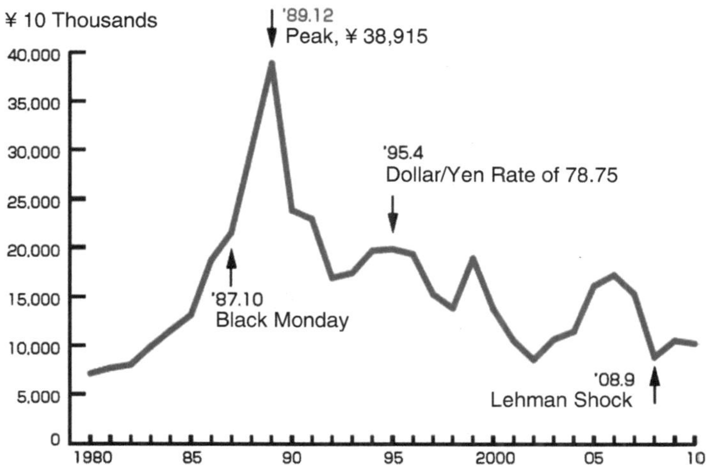

Fig. 1.8 Nikkei stock average

3.3 Use of Private-Sector Funds and the Optimal Mix of Public and Private Funds

Figure 1.9 shows the forms in which private and public monies are to be collected. Ideally, doing this with 100% private-sector funds would be most desirable. However, in the case of enterprises that have some degree of externality, such as solar power panels, it is conceivable that public funds (money from the national or local government) could be introduced in the form of matching funds or grants that would be combined with funds from private-sector investors to provide such enterprises with funding. In Fig. 1.9, private-sector funds are shown at 70% whilst the public-sector funds are 30%. This means that 70% consists of private-sector funding, and if we suppose that all the proceeds (the returns) from the investment project go to the private-sector investors, and if we assume that even though the profitability for the private-sector investors (i.e., their rate of return) may be slightly low, that profitability will increase if dividends do not have to be paid to the originators of the national government funds. To put this another way, the private-sector investors' profitability will rise to a rate of 100/70. This will make the investment attractive to private-sector investors because it will offer an anticipated rate of return higher than the benchmark profitability shown by the horizontal line in Fig. 1.10.

Combining private and public sector funds as described above can have a leveraging effect because, first, such a project can be presented to investors as having official government backing, and second, because even if the rate of return on the investment project is on the low side, interest and dividends will not need to be paid to the national government or to public agencies, which has the effect of raising the rate of return for private-sector investors. It is because of these two effects that it is

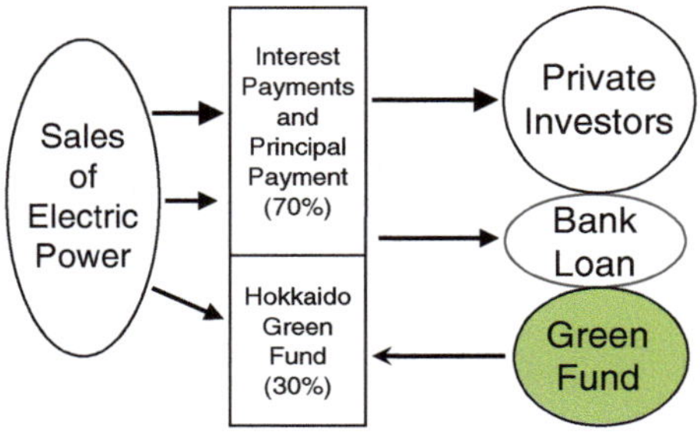

Fig. 1.9 Wind power trust fund of Japan

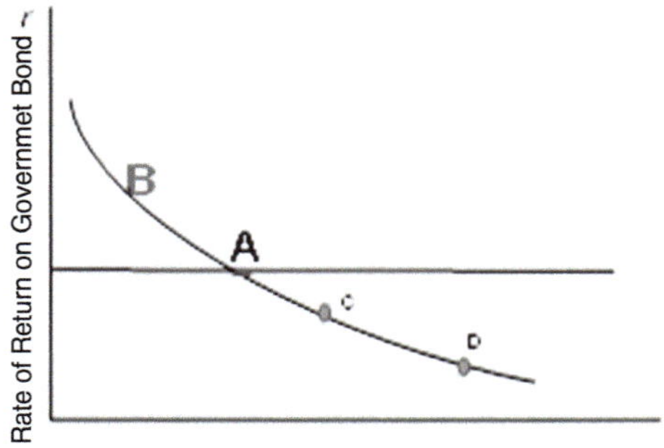

Fig. 1.10 Rate of return on each project

so important to combine private funds and public funds. A third reason is that the introduction of private-sector funds will eliminate sloppy and drawn-out construction work and will encourage greater project efficiency. The reason for this is that the private sector is always thinking about how to obtain its profit more quickly (Yoshino 2010).

The next point to consider is how to determine the proportional mix of public monies and private funds. The ideal approach would be to introduce enough national government funding that the rate of return on public-sector funds would be just about the same as the yield on government bonds. A second conceivable approach would be, in the case of an environmental project such as solar panels, to set the government funding to an amount determined by economic analysis corresponding to the economic savings resulting from the reduction in CO_2 or other such emissions.

3.4 *Necessity for Review of Investment Trust Fees*

When putting together approaches for funds of these kinds, it is necessary to consider improvements with respect to sales commissions, which are not functioning very well in the current state of investment trusts. The discussion here will refer to sales commissions for financial instruments.

Fig. 1.11 Sales of trust funds

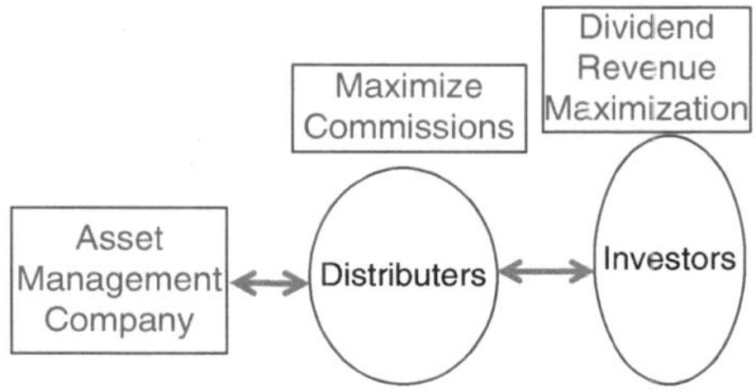

As matters stand at present, asset management companies have put together several different investment trusts. The asset management companies decide on sales commissions for the different investment trusts and pay commissions to the banks and post offices that sell them. The banks and securities companies that sell investment trusts see profits at their branches rise from sales of investment trusts that have high sales commissions. Ultimately, therefore, they tend to aim not to maximize dividends paid to investors, but rather to maximize their own income from commissions. Consequently, it may be the case that post offices and banks that sell investment trusts do not sell products that are necessarily favourable for investors.

In selling HIT funds, therefore, it seems most desirable that commissions for sales companies should be set at levels that are in proportion to the dividends distributed to investors. The fee structure could include a minimum fee applied to all products as an identical fixed fee. Then this could be combined with an additional dividend-linked fee (a variable fee) that varies with the amount of dividend distributed to the investor. Such a structure would encourage sales of financial instruments that give consideration to distribution to investors (see Fig. 1.11).

If this is not done, the banks, post offices, securities companies, and agricultural cooperatives that sell investment trusts may well end up selling only those investment trust products that pay the highest commission. One other important matter is that these asset management companies are expert evaluators, and they will be required to make firm decisions on which projects to select for hometown investments. It is also a distinctive characteristic of HIT funds that investors can see their investment in, for example, the operation of wind power generation, their returns, and other such aspects with their own eyes as they take part in the investment fund. These are funds that allow us to get an immediate feeling for the reality of the investment—to see its face, so to speak.

4 Stable Supply of Risk Capital in Japan and Asia

The same can probably be said about other parts of Asia. Like Japan, the rest of Asia has bank-centred financial systems, and though they offer micro credit, they loan out money at high interest rates, so that SMEs and other borrowers in Asia are having a hard time of it. It is truly essential that the HIT funds discussed here develop in Asia as investment alternatives to micro credit and venture capital. For infrastructure investment and other such large projects, it will also be possible in the future to put together funds in the form of infra funds (infrastructure investment trusts) and to implement project finance.

When collecting funds for HIT funds in Japan and other parts of Asia, there will be investment projects (such as roads and other infrastructure) that demand long-term funding. The question will be whether HIT funds can put together financing that will be stable for 5 years, 10 years, or even longer periods. In the United States and Europe, venture capital and other funds tend to operate in the short term. Money from life insurance companies and pension funds is best suited to stable funding for the long term. If private pension funds also begin to participate, then demand will emerge in tandem for long-term HIT funds as places for them to invest. In order to engage in long-term fund management, it will be necessary for Asia to provide for an increase, on the fund-providing side, in pension funds and life insurance companies that want long-term investment. In the case of Japan, it is necessary for pension funds and insurance companies to thoroughly assess the projects that will receive their investments as long-term HIT funds, such as infrastructure projects, and long-term hometown investments even as they expand the range of their investments.

5 Fostering Sound Hometown Investment Trust Funds

HIT funds, forest investment funds for environmental protection, infrastructure funds, and other such investments are expected to also appear in areas removed from the main urban centres. When they do, it will be necessary to prevent the rise of unscrupulous investment fund companies that offer empty talk about inferior projects for investment, have no commitment to the projects of the companies invested in, and lead investors into loss.

When HIT funds are on a small scale, it can be expected that many individual investors will consider the investment as support for the local region. They can be expected to consider the investment trust to operate as a combination of contribution and investment. A variety of different regional assistance funds have come into being, including HIT funds for the purpose of building fishing boats for fishermen who were victims of the Great East Japan Earthquake, and funds to support local shark fin enterprises.

The fund operators will have to set up a self-regulating organization that checks the activity of each other's fund and cultivates excellent operators who will not betray the confidence of investors. This is necessary otherwise the HIT funds that have finally managed to grow will lose their credibility, people will not want to invest again, and HIT funds will not expand. It will be necessary to monitor the self-regulating organization as it supports excellent operators and eliminates the unscrupulous. It will also be desirable to create a system whereby the Financial Services Agency or other government authority monitors investment funds as they do Type II Financial Instruments Business Operators and eliminates unscrupulous operators.

References

McNelis P, Yoshino N (2012) Macroeconomic volatility under high accumulation of government debt: lessons from Japan. Adv Complex Syst 15(Suppl 2):1250057. doi:10.1142/S0219525912500579

Revankar N, Yoshino N (2008) An empirical analysis of Japanese banking behavior in a period of financial instability. Keio Econ Stud 45(1):1–15

Yoshino N (2010) Financing transport infrastructure development in Southeast Asia. OECD, Southeast Asian economic outlook, 2010 November. OECD, Paris (Chapter 6)

Yoshino N (2012) Global imbalance and the development of capital flows among Asian countries. OECD J Financ Market Trends 1:81–112

Yoshino N, Hirano T (2011) Pro-cyclicality of the Basel capital requirement ratio and its impact on banks. Asian Econ Pap 10(2):22–36

Yoshino N, Mizoguchi T (2013) Changes in the flow of funds and the fiscal policy rules needed for fiscal stabilization. Public policy review 6(1), Ministry of Finance, Japan

Chapter 2
Supply of Risk Capital for Regional Development in Japan

Atsuo Akai

1 Overview

In this chapter, we indicate the limits of the present form of financial intermediation, and show how funds such as the Hometown Investment Trust (HIT) funds can point the way to the future. As Japan's domestic financial system has transitioned from a multi-layered to a single-layered form,[1] it has become clear that excessive reliance has been placed on indirect financing, which has reached its functional limit in financial intermediation. Despite over 10 years of discussions in various public–private forums, there has unfortunately been no significant change in the financial structure itself (Akai 2007a). Nevertheless, the direct–indirect responses to the international financial crisis of 2008 have given rise to several fascinating public–private initiatives for supporting local economies.

One example can be seen in the Ministry of Land, Infrastructure, Transport and Tourism's (MLIT) Project for Promoting the Supply of Non-recourse Loans Useful for Regional Urban Development, which was part of the government's fiscal 2009 financial crisis response. This endeavour was aimed at promoting local production and local consumption by financing community development with the resources of

[1] Japan's domestic banking system used to comprise three main types of institution: (1) government sponsored banks such as the Development Band of Japan, (2) long term credit banks and (3) city banks. This meant that Japan's indirect finance used to be characterised by differing funding formats for the lenders themselves which enabled a variety of risk return/duration targets. This is what is meant by "multi-layered" here. During the course of the last 10 years, Japan's financial system underwent reform, in the context of bad debt resolution and the general change of emphasis "from public to private." As a result, today, our indirect financing system has become "single-layered," i.e. dominated by city banks providing only relatively short funding/lending duration targets.

A. Akai (✉)
Morgan Stanley MUFG Securities, Tokyo, Japan

Waseda University, Tokyo, Japan
e-mail: a.akai@aoni.waseda.jp

N. Yoshino and S. Kaji (eds.), *Hometown Investment Trust Funds: A Stable Way to Supply Risk Capital*, DOI 10.1007/978-4-431-54309-1_2, © Springer Japan 2013

local financial institutions, and it can also be seen as a pioneering initiative leading to others in long-term finance.

The HIT funds platform supported mainly by the Regional Revitalization Bureau of the Cabinet Secretariat is another example. This initiative aims to encourage households to invest some of their savings in small-budget projects throughout the country.

This chapter describes specific efforts to create new financial flow frameworks, and considers the direction in which Japan's capital supply structure should develop.

2 New Developments in the Supply of Risk Capital in Real Estate and Infrastructure

2.1 Background

The real estate investment market, as an effective link between the real estate market, which has long been Japan's largest asset market, and domestic and overseas financial markets, can be said to have played major roles impacting this country's economy and society.

The real estate investment market, by playing its essential role in effectively linking real estate and finance, has made it possible to effectively apply private-sector capital to the renovation of the stock of public and private real estate and infrastructure developed in the post-war and high-economic-growth years, and the period up through today. It has supported the evolution of the domestic industrial structure to serve future needs through the revitalization of the cities that are collections of that public and private infrastructure, and provided financial support for various plans incorporating considerations of growth particularly in other parts of Asia. The real estate investment market has made possible the improvement of living environments and supported various other initiatives underpinning the real economy. At the same time, it has provided opportunities for the stable investment of domestic financial assets, said to be as great as 1,400 trillion yen, serving as a font of vigour for Japan's financing businesses and prosperity for its citizens.

However, whilst Japan's real estate investment market can be said to have grown significantly over the 10 years since its birth (Akai 2007b), as shown in Fig. 2.1, its scale has reached only 33 trillion (8 trillion yen of which is accounted for by real estate owned by J-REITs), even if real estate investment trusts, a form of securitization in the broad sense, are counted. The market, in other words, cannot be described as having achieved adequate scale, either as a financial market or as a real estate market. It is not yet capable of giving rise to new possibilities for Japan's 2,300 trillion yen stock of real estate, or acting as a broad, deep market offering responses to the many issues confronting the stock and real estate market (Akai 2009).

Real estate and finance are intimately connected to nearly every aspect of the national economy, and the relationship between the two could be called one of mutual dependence. The fate of approximately 80 % of corporate and personal finances, as direct or indirect collateral, is dependent on the value of real estate, and a sudden crash

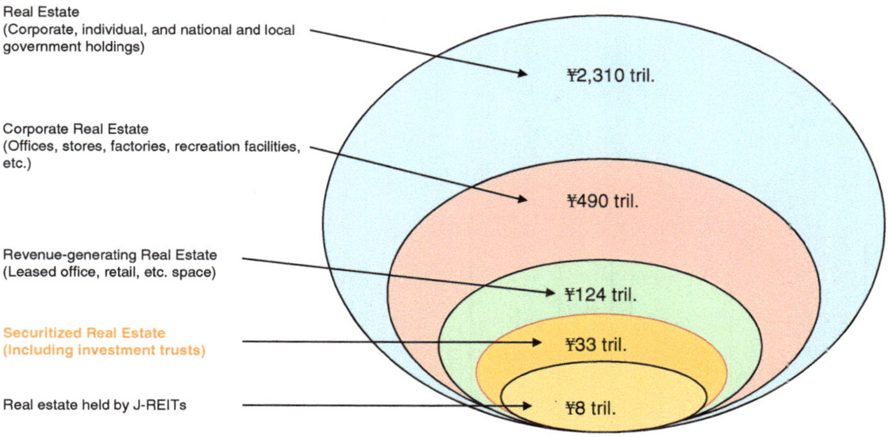

Fig. 2.1 Linking Japan's real estate and financial markets. *Source*: National Accounts Statistics for 2005; Ministry of Land, Infrastructure, Transport and Tourism (MLIT) survey data, Corporations Survey on Buildings (2003); Real Estate Securitization in Japan (MLIT 2006); Guide to Real Estate Securitization and Real Estate Finance, 2008, Morgan Stanley; 1998 Kokudo Hakusho (Land White Paper) MLIT

in real estate prices would have destabilizing effects on the financial system. It goes without saying, therefore, that in areas away from major cities stable supplies of capital from the financial system are indispensable for maintaining the values of real estate and the cities themselves, and updating functionalities; absent this capital, advancing initiatives for maintaining the competitiveness of cities would be impossible. What is more, real estate and urban infrastructure that have been allowed to degrade to the point of disfunctionality are a heavy burden on the national economy.

As is shown in Fig. 2.2, 30–40 % of the infrastructure of Japan's major cities was built between 1955 and 1975, during the nation's period of high economic growth. Adding to this the fact that new quake-resistance standards were introduced later, in 1981, only highlights the significance of this point.

Nevertheless, despite that this discussion has so far addressed what should be well-known facts, a common understanding of them—even as they emerged and took hold through the period of high economic growth, the bubble era, and the ensuing 20 years of economic stagnation—has yet to develop among the Japanese people.

When the global financial crisis struck in 2008, shrinking balance sheets among foreign financial institutions and greatly reduced business activity among the megabanks and other large domestic financial institutions resulted in a marked drop-off in capital inflows to the real estate market (see Fig. 2.3). Capital supply shortages were particularly acute for long-term, mezzanine, and other forms of risk capital, and it quickly became obvious that the regional financial institutions turned to as replacements for the foreign and domestic financial institutions that had pulled out, particularly in areas outside of Tokyo and other large metropolitan locales, were severely limited as stand-ins.

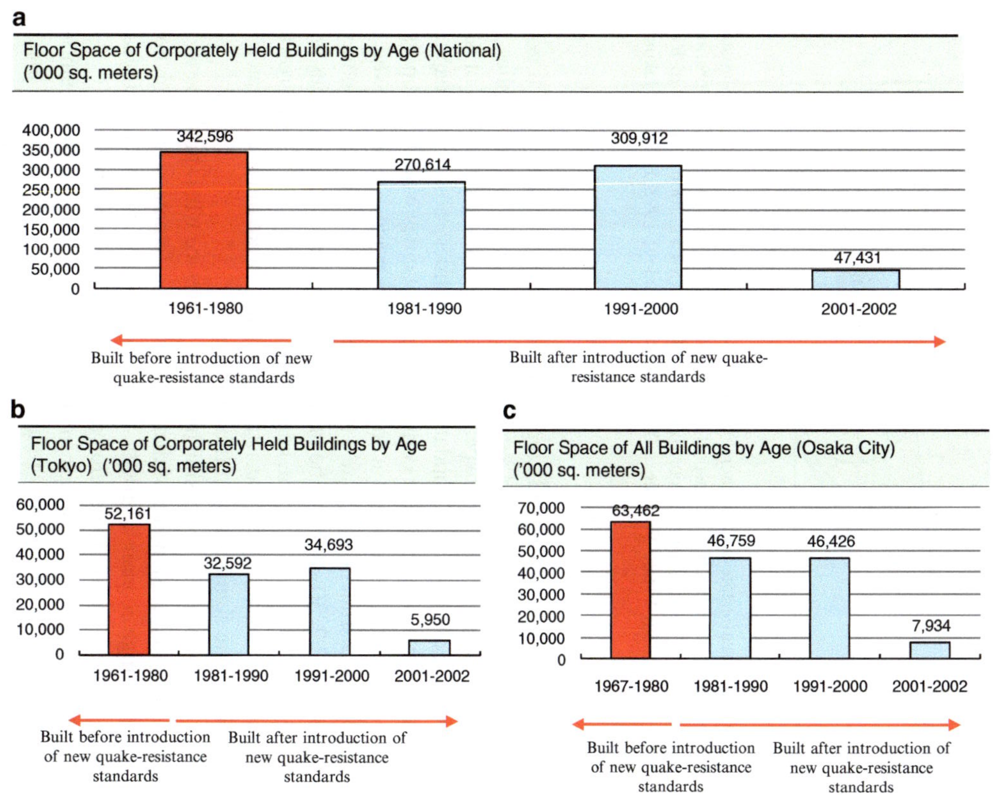

Fig. 2.2 Quake-resistance of decaying urban infrastructure. Floor space of corporately held buildings by age in (**a**) national, (**b**) Tokyo. *Source*: MLIT's corporations survey on buildings 2003. *Note*: This data is for buildings outside of manufacturing plant sites and excludes structures used for housing employees, rental residential property, and buildings located on land held for sale (inventory assets). (**c**) Floor space of all buildings by age (Osaka City). *Source*: Osaka City. *Note*: Data for 1980 and earlier is based on a calendar year, data for 1981 and later is based on a fiscal year

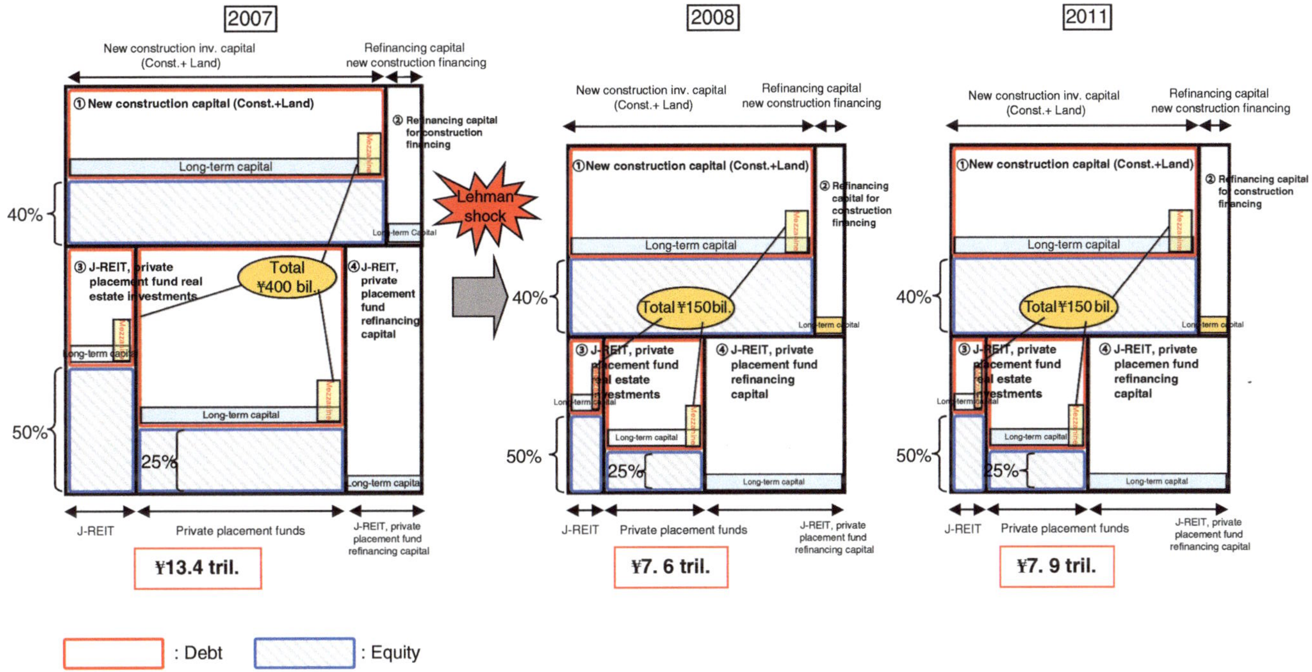

Fig. 2.3 Real estate sector capital inflows. Prepared by author in 2010 based on material from the Expert Board on Urban Redevelopment Policy

2.2 Initiatives Focused on Urban Growth Strategies

The government's growth strategies for major cities, issued after the change in ruling parties in 2009, revealed the new administration's perception of the problems confronting Japan's major cities. That view, whilst acknowledging that these cities had led Japan's growth in the past, focused on the fact that other national governments were pursuing initiatives aimed at enhancing the competitiveness of cities like Seoul, Singapore, Shanghai, and Tianjin and concluded that Japan's lack of national strategies to develop cities from international and regional perspectives could result in even Tokyo succumbing to the combined impacts of a falling birth rate and aging population, and growth of the nation as a whole being undermined. It went on to posit that Japan, too, must strategically pursue investment to construct or improve airports, seaports, roads, and other critical infrastructure from which high returns could be expected, and create hubs for the movement of people and goods internationally and within Asia (Akai 2010; Secretariat of the Urban Renaissance Headquarters 2011).

With that direction having been set, the 2011 complete overhaul of the government's Basic Policies for Urban Renaissance called for all sectors of the national government to cooperate in the development of urban strategies that would work to strengthen the nation's international competitiveness, the effective use of private expertise and capital through Public Private Partnership (PPP), Private Finance Initiative (PFI), and New Public Commons initiatives aimed at advancing the necessary urban renaissance policies, and the development of a financing environment that would enable the stable provision of the capital needed for urban renaissance (Secretariat of the Urban Renaissance Headquarters 2011).[2]

This was the first time that a coherent treatment of the financing environment was included in the Basic Policies for Urban Renaissance, which have traditionally focused only on matters directly related to infrastructure construction, and the stage for that development was set by the understanding of financing environment matters, as discussed above.

Furthermore, as the debate surrounding revision of the Basic Policies for Urban Renaissance proceeded, the Financial Services Agency (FSA) revealed in its Action Plan for the New Growth Strategy (2010) a policy more interventionist than any previously adopted by a Japanese financial regulator. It said, in short that the FSA would, in view of the work underway to revise the Basic Policies for Urban Renaissance, take positive steps to both promote the acquisition, redevelopment, development, etc. of real estate, and invigorate the real estate investment market.

Meanwhile, at the MLIT, a committee established to consider matters related to real estate investment market strategies (a private advisory body to the MLIT Minister) made specific recommendations in five areas for creating appropriate connections between the real estate and financial markets, and making the real estate investment market into an active venue for advancing urban redevelopment and infrastructure

[2]Please see the chapter on"Establishment of a Financing Environment for Promoting Stable Private-Sector Urban Development."

renewal, in its final report (MLIT 2010). These five areas consisted of: (1) Debt markets, (2) J-REIT markets, (3) The private placement fund market, (4) The real estate market, and (5) The real estate investment market and systems for financial flows.

It is these kinds of developments at interested government ministries and agencies that contributed to the development of the common understanding of issues concerning a financial system for real estate and infrastructure that, over the 2009–2010 period, served as a basis for the identification of structural problems in various governmental committees, public and private discussions crossing traditional organizational boundaries, action at various government ministries and agencies, and, ultimately, the concrete public–private initiatives we see today.

2.3 Supply of Non-recourse Real Estate Loans by Regional Financial Institutions

As mentioned earlier, through 2008 and 2009, the market for non-recourse real estate loans was hit hard by the negative impact (rapidly widening spreads and declining liquidity) of the financial crisis on Commercial Mortgage-Backed Securities (CMBS) market, which in turn caused foreign financial institutions to pull out of the market. As prominent was the significant retrenching that megabanks and other domestic financial institutions implemented in their strategies. Furthermore, even the domestic and foreign institutions that continued to provide non-recourse loans on a limited basis were seen preparing for even greater problems in the securitization market. They did this by restricting collateral to large office buildings that were located in Tokyo or other major metro areas and easy to appraise.

The implications of those developments fell particularly hard on commercial buildings located in relatively large regional cities and cities, like those with bullet train stations, with concentrated city centres. These properties were located in prime areas favoured by tenants like branches of major banks, could expect relatively stable local tenant demand, and were seen as prime properties that could look forward to steady cash flows. In addition, amid the heated non-recourse lending competition that went on in Tokyo and other major cities beginning in 2005, these properties attracted the attention of foreign financial institutions and megabanks as balanced-risk-return lending opportunities. As non-recourse loans backed by these revenue-generating regional properties gained popularity for securitization, even the regional real estate firms handling transactions for these prime properties began taking out non-recourse loans.

Most of the non-recourse loans that had been provided, however, were for short periods of only about 3 years, so large volumes of these loans had to be refinanced as, or after, the impacts of the financial crisis peaked in 2008. Despite that their collateral meant steady cash flow from rent for the time being, borrowers faced a worsening lack of lenders willing to lend to them and, without the possibility of refinancing, lenders began auctioning off buildings to recover their loan funds.

Against the background of this worsening financing environment, attention turned to the possibility of strengthening the non-recourse real estate lending capabilities of regional financial institutions operating in areas where collateral properties were located, so that they could provide loans for refinancing.

However, notwithstanding the fact that many regional financial institutions had been investing in securitization products since the emergence of the CMBS market, almost none had experience or expertise in creating or implementing systems for originating non-recourse real estate loans, much less packaging loans as securitized products and selling them to other investors on the market.

When engaging in the making of non-recourse loans with securitization in mind, it is competitively advantageous to form large loan portfolios diversified geographically and by property type to gain a high credit rating for the end-product CMBS. And the larger the securitization pool, the lower will be the various fixed cost burdens. Considering the conditions regional financial institutions faced in terms of, for example, property sizes and numbers, rather than becoming a non-recourse lender, it made greater business sense to participate in the market as an investor in certain classes of CMBSs consisting of securitized non-recourse loans originated and packaged by third parties—major domestic or foreign financial institutions. This appears to have been the force driving regional financial institutions to invest in, rather than offer, CMBSs.

On the regulatory side, the financial crisis drew attention to the importance of ensuring traceability for the assets backing securitised products, and that in turn drove discussions in the FSF (Financial Stability Forum), at the request of the G7, and IOSCO's (International Organization of Securities Commissions) subprime taskforce. In Japan, discussions such as these led the FSA to revise its Comprehensive Guidelines for Supervision of Financial Instruments Business Operators in April 2008. Afterward, the Standard Information Reporting Package (SIRP), after review by a working group of the Japan Securities Dealers Association (JSDA), was announced [interim (July 2008) and final (March 2009) reports] together with the JSDA's Regulations Concerning Distributions, etc. of Securitized Products. The SIRP was developed as a way to standardize information on underlying assets for, and risks concerning, securitized products.

The SIRP was created to help investors in securitized products gain a firm grasp of, and manage, risks related to these products. However, based on the idea that it could also be used to identify and assess risks for the making of non-recourse loans that were the subject of securitisations, the same format was used in an effort to encourage regional financial institutions to take the place of foreign financial institutions and megabanks and use their stable local deposit-based funds to originate non-recourse loans backed by local real estate. As described above, regional financial institutions had had only indirect or limited involvement with non-recourse real estate loans until that time, as investors in securitised products.

This effort took the form of the MLIT's project for promoting the supply of non-recourse loans useful for regional urban development (MLIT 2009; Urban Renewal Coordinator Association of Japan 2008) and, as shown in Fig. 2.4, it involved multiple regional financial institutions making non-recourse real estate loans within the uniform SIRP-compliant framework. These loans would then be packaged via an SPC established with subordinated debt financing from the fund for increasing the

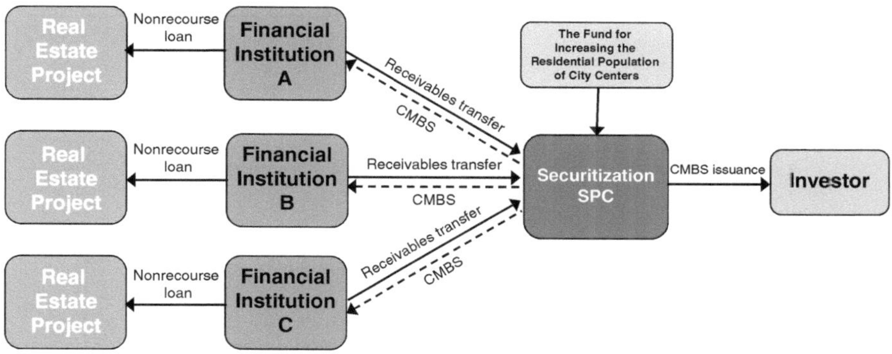

Fig. 2.4 Nonrecourse loan supply scheme involving regional financial institutions. *Source*: Regarding implementation of the project for promoting the supply of nonrecourse loans useful for regional urban development and the recruiting of arrangers (Chiho no machizukuri ni yakudatsu nonrikosuron kyokyu sokushin jigyou no jishi oyobi arenja boshu ni tsuite) (MLIT public relations materials, April 2009)

residential population of city centres (MLIT), and then sold as CMBSs to regional financial institutions[3] and other investors to raise capital.

This MLIT project, by not only adopting the already publicly announced SIRP but also promoting standardization of credit research terms and conditions and various contract procedures, sought to minimize the administrative and management burdens (hurdles) for regional financial institutions just getting into the business of nonrecourse lending. This endeavour can be viewed as the commercial real estate version of the RMBS operations based on the Japan Housing Finance Agency's Flat 35 and other such home loan products. The idea of creating financial instruments out of large pools of individual loans all originated under a standard framework, and selling them to institutional investors was widespread in Europe and, in Japan, shared characteristics with covered bonds, serious consideration of which took place later.

The MLIT project itself, as a part of the response to the financial crisis, lasted only 1 year. However, its basic concepts can be praised as leading to the framework that would encourage regional financial institutions interested in invigorating local economies to take positive action supporting the idea of raising and using capital locally.

2.4 New Initiatives in the Area of Public Infrastructure

Amid the discussions surrounding recovery from the Great East Japan Earthquake, which happened in March 2011, are ongoing debates of various topics related to the

[3]There was an expectation that regional financial institutions, by investing in CMBSs backed by nonrecourse loans originated by multiple regional financial institutions, could diversify away earthquake and other area-bias risks in their nonrecourse loan portfolios.

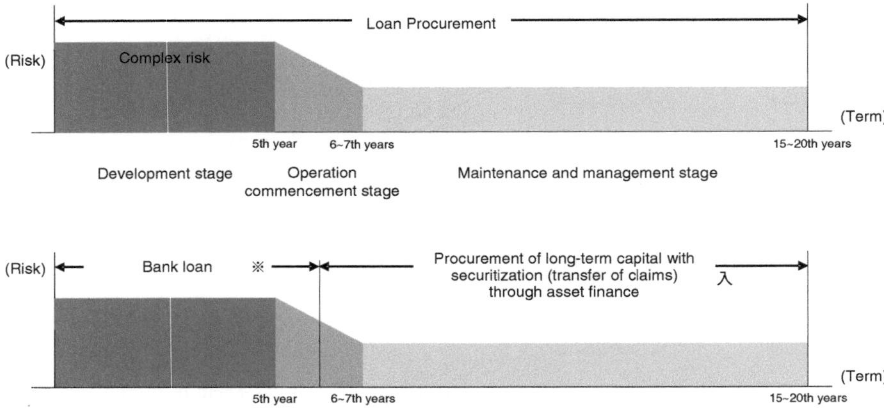

Fig. 2.5 PFI issues. (*Top*) Traditional PFI financing relying on bank financing; (*bottom*) application of private capital from various sources (separation of capital procurement into development and post-stabilization stages, and diversification of post-stabilization capital procurement through transfer of claims). (*Asterisk*) Bank can allocate funds obtained through refinancing to new projects

restoration of real estate and infrastructure, and new construction. Key points from the perspective of the multilinearisation of the financial system include the revision of PFI-related systems and consideration of the adoption of financial instruments based on the new (in Japan) concept of revenue bonds.

PFIs had been used mainly to expand the use of private capital to fund public infrastructure, like schools, hospitals, airports, and roads, by making it easier for investors to deal with various procedures. The history of their use, however, shows a significant decline in project numbers after peaking in 2008, and no growth in aggregate project value, which has remained around 3.2 trillion yen since the end of fiscal 2009. In these and other ways, therefore, use of the PFI approach has not developed as anticipated. Blame for this has been pinned on the limited long-term financing capability of existing indirect financial institutions, and consideration of how channels for long-term capital from external sources might be widened by, for example, facilitating the transfer of PFI bonds, is now underway.

In more concrete terms, the traditional approach of relying on funds procured through a single syndicated loan from a single financial institution (bank) through the entirety of the long period covered by a PFI would be replaced by loan capital provided in two stages—the development stage and the stable operation stage. This is described in Fig. 2.5. Under this concept, a bank would handle financing for the development stage, and deal with the relatively complex risk involved. For the subsequent longer, stable operation stage, the bank could apply asset finance or another such approach to transfer the loan to a life insurance company, or domestic or oversees pension fund. Ways of establishing conditions that would allow the promotion of such an efficient capital recovery approach are being considered and revised guidelines toward that end are expected to be issued by the end of fiscal 2012.

As for revenue bonds, which had not previously been used in Japan, the Special Provisions of Acts Related to National Tax, in Relation to Victims, etc. of the Great East Japan Earthquake authorized the issuance of revenue-linked bonds by public corporations owned in their entirety by local governments or by SPCs for infrastructure projects related to recovery from the Great East Japan Earthquake. These bonds are now being issued to secure capital from market sources interested in the profitability of toll roads, public housing, and other public infrastructure (FSA 2012b). In the US, which has a long history of issuing revenue bonds, the construction of Yankee Stadium was financed with this form of debt, which constitutes 66 % of local government bonds. In Japan, there are high expectations for the influx of capital from foreign public pension and infrastructure funds with experience investing in this area and for the participation of domestic long-term investors and regional financial institutions encouraged by their examples. Though revenue bonds were only recently introduced on a trial basis to aid the recovery of areas damaged the Great East Japan Earthquake, there is great potential for their use throughout Japan in linking the securing of capital for local infrastructure projects and capital investment by regional financial institutions. The use of revenue bonds would make it possible to enlist a private investment framework as a check on the soundness of infrastructure projects, accurately determine the extent of risk that could be borne by the private sector, and identify the point from which public assistance is required. And that understanding underpinning a clear division of public and private roles could help to advance the efficient allocation of capital.

2.5 Issues to Consider Going Forward

The discussion above has looked at issues and initiatives concerning the structure of capital flows in the areas of real estate and infrastructure in Japan, and it seems obvious that there is no room for questioning the ongoing need for strategic initiatives aimed at achieving a unified public–private structure for appropriately linking the real estate and infrastructure markets with financial markets. One such initiative, the project for promoting the supply of non-recourse loans useful for regional urban development, which promotes the application of the regional financial institution framework for locally raising and locally using capital to invigorate regional cities, can be viewed as a pioneering example for the future construction of public and private collaborative frameworks.

It is imperative that neither the economic measures taken to address the financial crisis that began with the subprime loan problem, nor the various initiatives that are aimed at promoting flows of private capital into urban development/redevelopment projects and only came into consideration to aid recovery from the Great East Japan Earthquake, be treated as temporary initiatives. To the contrary, they must be viewed as important steps leading to sustainable structural reform initiatives for the nation's system of capital flows.

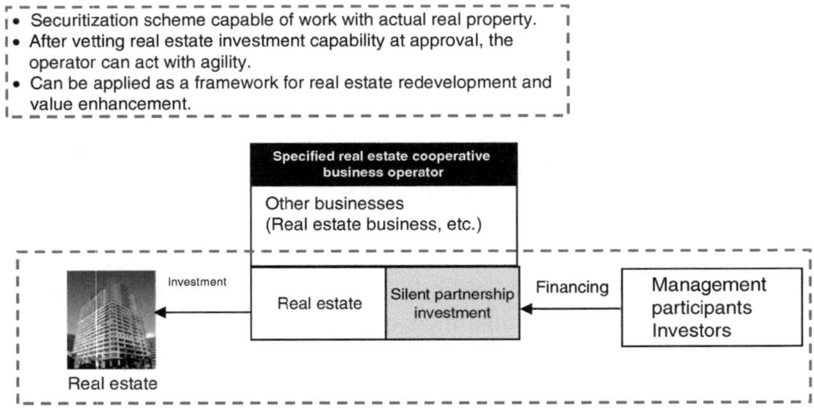

⟨Issues and Needed Action⟩

- Without the ability to separate assets of non-specified businesses and operators, risks (bankruptcy, etc.) from the operator's other businesses is borne, driving away institutional investors.
- Capital requirement for approval (¥100 mil.), installation of an administrative manager, and the inability to make use of a bankruptcy-remote SPC.
- Legal revision for implementation of a bankruptcy remoteness scheme is needed.

Fig. 2.6 Redevelopment of real estate and infrastructure via the real estate specified joint enterprise act framework

In this sense, the initiatives that are aimed at promoting flows of private capital into real estate and infrastructure areas in need of redevelopment (which cannot be discussed here for lack of space) (Fig. 2.6), and would result from the Real Estate Specified Joint Enterprise Act revisions currently under consideration, should be treated as important framework initiatives for the construction of sustainable financial intermediation channels that would serve real estate and infrastructure redevelopment needs throughout the country going forward, even if they are now seen as approaches for funding disaster recovery. Future application policies that should be considered based on the above assessment are discussed below.

3 The Role of HIT Funds (Small Investments Aimed at Regional Development)

3.1 Concept and Basic Framework

Hometown Investment Trust Funds (small investments aimed at regional development), by creating a new financial intermediary channel outside the indirect financing and market sectors of Japan's financial system, as discussed in Sect. 1, also create a flow

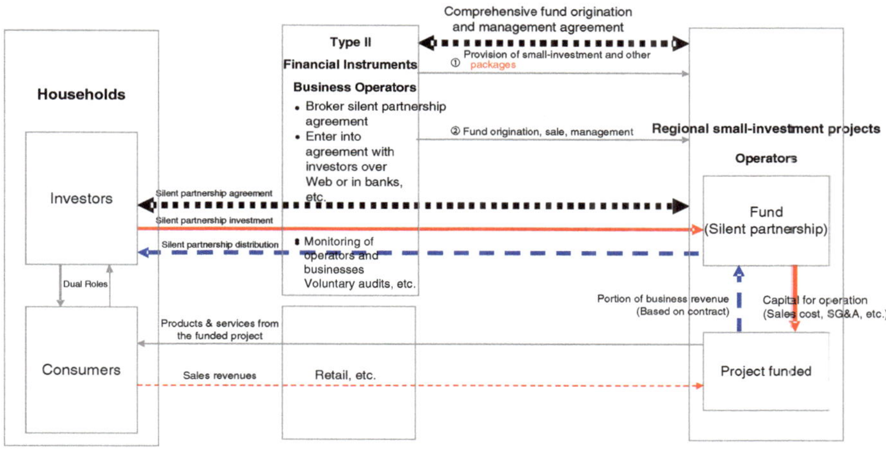

Fig. 2.7 Basic Hometown Investment Trust Funds (small investments aimed at regional development) scheme. Prepared by the author based on information provided by the Hometown Investment Trust Funds Platform Promotion Committee and Music Securities

of funds with a new risk return profile—a flow that cannot be provided by the current indirect financing system alone—and a financing scheme based on a new concept that attempts to strengthen the functions of finance as a system supporting the real economy. That basic concept is depicted in Fig. 2.7.

A description of HIT Funds would begin with its being a new capital supply channel that, as small-scale investment bypassing financial institution balance sheets, can mobilize risk tolerance different from that of banks and other financial institutions and personal will, both of which are embodied in household financial assets.

When a bank takes in deposits from individuals, the fundamental nature of deposits (the need to guarantee principal and the fact that deposits mature) forces it to invest conservatively and mainly for short terms, given the need to have funds available for maturing deposits (most of which are short-term). On the other hand, for individuals acting on their own, prohibitively high transaction costs have until recently made direct investment in projects impractical. The proliferation of the Internet, however, with low-cost electronic approaches, is now beginning to make it possible for individuals to invest directly in projects in need of capital, and do so without changing the risk characteristics of personal financial assets. Hometown Investment Trust Funds, therefore, are a financing scheme made possible in part by this kind of technological advancement.

Use of the silent partnership approach in the interest of management independence for the investee is another, major, characteristic of hometown investment. On this point, it differs in the extreme from traditional investments in partnerships and common stock. In contrast with these approaches, which are synonymous with allowing participation in the management of an investment project (despite the slight possibility of little real impact without large percentage investments), silent partnership investments, like other securitized transactions, allow for investment in individual projects, and this, from the project management perspective, offers the advantage of being able to secure capital whilst maintaining management independence. There is also this. Most individual investors are company or government employees and are not permitted to engage in other income-generating occupations. Given that investments in partnerships are often assumed to include management participation, an opportunity to investment via a silent partnership should significantly lower the hurdle for individual investors.

A third major distinguishing characteristic of HIT Funds is that ongoing relationships between investees and investors often result in the conversion of investors into consumers (fans) for the investee—something not often seen with other forms of financing (both investing and lending). From the project management point of view, HIT funds, therefore, mean the ability to not only procure capital but also secure new customers.

3.2 Issues Going Forward

Several issues must be considered before hometown investment (small investments aimed at invigorating local economies) can be promoted in earnest.

First on the list is boosting awareness of hometown investment as a financial instrument and putting it on an equal footing with other financial instruments in terms of tax treatment. This includes consideration of the possibility of pooling hometown investment gains and losses with those of stocks, bonds, and other financial instruments.

High-level regulation aimed at protecting investors, who will consist mainly of individuals, will clearly also be necessary. This is the second item on the list and would include consideration of matters like standardization of approaches that would facilitate the identification of investment risks for individual investors, and the development of disclosure (project reports) systems and formats; the adoption of the Type II Financial Instruments Firms Association's self-regulation rules regarding information reporting and disclosure; and systems for excluding malicious operators aiming to engage in fraudulent transactions and for receiving complaints. In addition, because of the impracticality of strictly separating, under the existing silent partnership investment framework, business risk associated with the operators of projects receiving investment from risks associated with the projects themselves, it will be important to continuously improve the investment system and devise new approaches as necessary.

Ways to improve convenience for individual investors, to go along with the investor protections discussed above, should also be considered. Specific examples of this third item would include the ability to pool gains and losses as mentioned above, the development of systems for accepting investment applications at retail banking and other such facilities for elderly, affluent, or other individual investors who might prefer not to use the Internet to make investments, and the implementation of tax benefits [for example, the creation of a system (linked to the local tax collection system) for using local tax revenue refunds to partially cover losses] for investments in projects designated by local governments as beneficial for regional economic invigoration.

On the other side of the coin, it will also be important to devise ways to make hometown investment an advantageous funding option for project operators and to attract outstanding projects as funding candidates. Regarding this fourth point, the inclusion of silent partnership investments meeting certain conditions in subordinated capital has already been addressed through an inspection manual revision the FSA undertook with the needs of areas hit by last year's disasters in mind. There is still a need, however, to consider detailed system design innovations that make the most of good intentions. An example would be revision of the tax treatment of the contribution portion (contributions are currently treated as taxable income for project operators) of the small funds combining investments and contributions [e.g. funds that are intended to support the recoveries of businesses in disaster areas (discussed in Chap. 3)] that have been created especially to provide capital to businesses in disaster-stricken areas.

Looking ahead to the nationwide adoption of HIT Funds, measures to encourage participation by regional financial institutions and other parties that would excel as system participants constitutes a fifth point. Adding promising investment candidates on a regional basis in particular by enhancing the assessment capabilities of regional financial institutions is especially important and points to the need to consider policy support measures for linking to relationship banking and other such programs.

Hopes are that the HIT Funds will grow as an original Japanese financial industry cluster, as action on various issues like these is taken.

3.3 Possibilities for Expanding from Small-Scale Investment in Business to Infrastructure Finance

Until this point, this discussion has focused on the basic ideas and issues to consider for future development of HIT funds as a scheme for direct investment by individuals via silent partnerships. Looking to the future, however, it would appear that hometown investment should not be limited to the provision of small amounts of business investment.

The following chapters describe various business investment examples. One is a sake brewery fund that has collected capital through a silent partnership and then provided this capital to sake breweries to procure rice, a raw material. As a result of last year's disasters, however, some breweries suffered severe damage to the structures housing their operations. Capital to procure raw material, therefore, would be insufficient for restarting their businesses, so money was also allocated for the construction of temporary structures and this played a critical role in getting these businesses back on their feet.

Going forward, there appears to be a need to consider schemes that, in addition to simple business investment (financing), would also allow investment

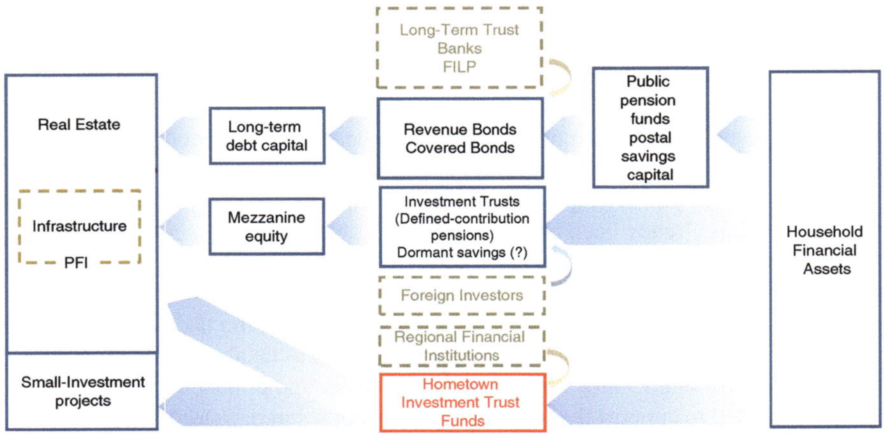

Fig. 2.8 Future of Japan's capital supply structure

(financing) for combinations of equipment/facilities and real estate to address needs like that described above. Application of the Real Estate Specified Joint Enterprise Act framework mentioned in Sect. 2 may be an effective course of action for the development of such schemes. If that framework could be applied as a scheme for direct investment (financing) by individual investors in small-scale infrastructure projects, it is conceivable that equity investment could be provided by local governments, subordinated financing (mezzanine) by individual investors, and senior debt by regional financial institutions in a division of roles that makes the most of the unique characteristics of each investor type to create a regional capital flow structure.

4 The Road Ahead

The discussion above has examined the need to build a multi-linear financial intermediation system to supplement Japan's traditional financial system, and various initiatives, including ongoing ones, that have been pursued over the previous 10-plus years (Fig. 2.8).

It is clear that Japan's real estate and infrastructure sectors require stable supplies of long-term and mezzanine capital for redevelopment and updating. Considering that the banking sector's financial intermediation function will continue to be limited in its ability to meet these demands, there will be an ongoing need to strategically strengthen the real estate investment market—in particular its long-term and mezzanine capital supply capability—as a market finance system supplementing the banking sector.

Discussions of PFIs and revenue bonds, covered bonds (FSA 2012a), and the development of a non-recourse loan market should also be pursued within the context of approaches for reinforcing an integrated system of the type mentioned above.

In addition, HIT Funds, as a third capital intermediation channel able to tap into household financial assets, could become an original Japanese small-investment scheme based on recent financial innovations and aiming to supplement the capital supply capability of Japan's traditional financial system. Positioning HIT funds as a stable source of capital for invigorating local economies, there is a need, from the perspective of designing future systems, to incorporate hometown investment in new financial industry business models and to pursue steady initiatives aimed at financial business growth through the geographic expansion of hometown investment.

Moving forward, the public and private sectors should act in unison to continue building a sustainable growth model for a new Japanese financial system, whilst also enhancing the capital supply capabilities of the domestic financial system, which underpins the real economy.

References

Akai A (2007a) Lessons from world financial crisis and opportunity for Japanese asset-finance market: as a unique local market model to support real economy. Ann Soc Econ Stud Securities 45:146–151

Akai A (2007b) The transformation of Japan's financial market and the future of the real estate securitization business. CMBS World, pp. 20–27 and p. 63

Akai A (2009) Japanese asset-finance market and property market data: recent developments and future. J Prop Assess Policy (20):1–8

Akai A (2010) Financial framework to support projects on renewal of urban functions in the new international economic environment. Keidanren Trend, pp. 32–35

Financial Services Agency (2012a) The action plan for the new growth strategy, December 2010. http://www.fsa.go.jp/news/22/sonota/20101224-5.html. Accessed 31 Oct 2012

Financial Services Agency (2012b) Publication of taxation of revenue bonds Q&A. http://www.fsa.go.jp/news/23/sonota/20120529-1.html. Accessed 31 Oct 2012

Japan Securities Dealers Association (2009) Working group on distributions of securitized products: final report, March 2009. http://www.jsda.or.jp/shiryo/houkokusyo/h21/shoukenka_wg_final.html. Accessed 31 Oct 2012

Ministry of Land, Infrastructure, Transport and Tourism (MLIT) (2006) Real estate securitization in Japan. MLIT's press release of December 2006. http://www.mlit.go.jp/kisha/kisha06/03/031212_2_.html; http://www.mlit.go.jp/kisha/kisha06/03/031219_.html. Accessed 31 Oct 2012

Ministry of Land, Infrastructure, Transport and Tourism (MLIT) (2009) Implementation of the project for promoting the supply of non-recourse loans for regional urban development and call for arrangers. MLIT's press release of April 2009. http://www.mlit.go.jp/report/press/house06_hh_000024.html. Accessed 31 Oct 2012

Ministry of Land, Infrastructure, Transport and Tourism (MLIT) (2010) Report of the committee on real estate investment market strategy. http://www.mlit.go.jp/totikensangyo/const/sosei_const_tk3_000018.html. Accessed 31 Oct 2012

Secretariat of the Urban Renaissance Headquarters, Cabinet Secretariat (2011) Basic policies for urban renaissance, totally revised edition. http://www.toshisaisei.go.jp/kihonhoushin_kaitei/zenmenkaitei.pdf Accessed 31 Oct 2012

Urban Renewal Coordinator Association of Japan (2008) Report by the study group concerning the market development of the non-recourse loans for regional urban development

Chapter 3
Hometown Investment Trust Funds in Japan

Masami Komatsu

Keeping with the theme of "Hometown Investment Trust (HIT) funds in Japan," in this chapter we focus mainly on the initiatives of our company, Music Securities.

We provide some examples of micro-investment corresponding to HIT funds (small investments aimed at regional development) and our "Securité Disaster Area Support Funds[1]" to recover from natural catastrophes.

1 Overview of the Use and Basic Structure of the HIT Scheme

1.1 Outline of Usage Example

First, the basic scheme of "hometown investment trust funds" (small investments aimed at regional development) is that they are small-lot (micro) investments made through contracts with silent partnerships as described by Professor Atsuo Akai in Chap. 2. Since our company was established in the year 2000 it has been using micro-investment schemes through silent partnerships to assist in the fundraising of businesses throughout the nation, and we have built up a track record as a micro-investment platform.

[1] The name of this fund has so far been translated in more ways than one. The World Bank (2011) called it the "Japan Earthquake Securité Supporting Fund" while the United Nations (2012) refers to it as "Disaster Site Support Fund." Others categorise this fund under the broader name of "Earthquake Relief Fund." The name used in this text is a direct translation of the Japanese name, reflecting the name of our company, Music Securities.

M. Komatsu (✉)
Music Securities Inc., Tokyo, Japan
e-mail: komatsu@musicsecurities.com

N. Yoshino and S. Kaji (eds.), *Hometown Investment Trust Funds: A Stable Way to Supply Risk Capital*, DOI 10.1007/978-4-431-54309-1_3, © Springer Japan 2013

Table 3.1 Main areas of business of the funds

Type	Number of funds	Total fund offering per fund	Project details
Music	60	500,000 yen to 77.39 million yen	Manufacture and sales of music CDs
Junmaisyu sake brewing	19	4.4–33.35 million yen	Brewing and sales of junmaisyu sake
Developing nations support	6	28.5–52.92 million yen	Aimed at overseas microfinancing institutions
Agriculture and forestry	6	8.88–49.4 million yen	Production and sale of rice, rearing free-range pigs,, forestry operations and lumber sales
Sports	1	52.96 million yen	Operation of J-League team
Disaster area support	37	7–100 million yen	Disaster area restoration

As of August 2012, 69 companies have used the scheme, and the number of funds has reached 166 (of which 89 are still under offer or operating, and 77 have been redeemed). The total subscription amount is approximately 2.8 billion yen, and we have around 50,000 registered members.

In terms of fund redemption results, as of August 2012, the number of redeemed funds (of which the term has expired) was 77, and the number of funds in which the return was lower than the initial capital funding was 13.

Table 3.1 provides an outline of the main areas of business of the funds. The most numerous are music funds which we have dealt with since the establishment of our business, with 60 funds having been set up. The total amount of each fund varies, with the smallest fund raising 500,000 yen for the production of a CD mini album and the largest fund raising 77.39 million yen per album. The funds are used for recording costs, advertising and packaging costs, and so on. In addition to the music funds, we have also set up funds for the production of *junmaisyu* sake (a superior type of sake using no distilled alcohol), for overseas aid in developing counties (as explained in Chap. 4), for agriculture and forestry, for the operation of the Tokyo Verdi J-League professional football team, and for the provision of assistance in disaster areas.

Over the past three fiscal years the track record of our securitisation division, which is the department in our company in charge of micro-investment, has seen a 4.5 times increase in the funding amount, a doubling of sales, and a doubling of operating profits.

1.2 Investor Attributes and Investment Motives

The results of a questionnaire completed by 20,000 of our investors shows their attributes and investment motives. Table 3.2 shows the investors' gender and age. Whilst there are still more male (66%) than female (33%) investors, the number of female investors has been rising since the establishment of the Securité Disaster Area Support

Table 3.2 Gender and age distribution of investors

	Male (%)	Female (%)
Age group	66.85	33.15
20–29	14.84	15.80
30–39	32.88	32.81
40–49	24.37	23.91
50–59	14.41	15.31
60–69	10.30	9.08
70–79	1.86	1.59
Invalid response/other	1.35	1.50
Total	100.00	100.00

Valid response, 20,000

Table 3.3 Occupational distribution of investors

Company employee	34.78%
Public servant	2.99%
Company director	2.59%
Self employed	6.08%
Housewife	5.56%
Student	7.65%
Part-time employee	4.04%
Other	8.27%
Invalid response	28.04%
Total	100.00%

Valid response, 20,000

Funds. In terms of age, the largest group of investors is in the 30s and 40s age bracket. It seems that as the investments are Internet-based, the dominant age groups reflect the age of the Internet users. Table 3.3 shows the breakdown of investors by occupation. The dominant group is company employees (34%), but students account for 7%. As a single lot in a fund can be bought for as little as 10,000 yen we are drawing investments from a wide range of people and students. The distribution of investors by prefecture is shown in Table 3.4. Miyagi Prefecture displays a high level of investment in relation to the size of its population, probably indicating the wish of its residents to support their local area in the wake of the 2011 earthquake disaster.

The motives for investing can be seen in Fig. 3.1. The dominant motives are a wish to support the businesses and a feeling of empathy for the businesses, along with a large number of people who respond positively to the micro-investment mechanism itself. One interesting feature is the extremely small number of people who cited the prospect of making a profit as their motivation for investing.

1.3 The Basic Mechanism of the Fund

I will now explain the basic mechanism of the fund using Fig. 3.2.

As a Type II Financial Instruments Business Operators registered by the Financial Services Agency, our company enters into an operating agreement with

Table 3.4 Prefectural distribution

Hokkaido	5.31%	Shiga	0.88%
Aomori	0.65%	Kyoto	2.04%
Iwate	0.94%	Osaka	7.22%
Miyagi	3.25%	Hyogo	4.12%
Akita	0.51%	Nara	0.89%
Yamagata	0.56%	Wakayama	0.46%
Fukushima	0.73%	Tottori	0.38%
Ibaraki	1.70%	Shimane	0.34%
Tochigi	0.98%	Okayama	1.43%
Gunma	0.95%	Hiroshima	1.37%
Saitama	6.00%	Yamaguchi	0.66%
Chiba	5.45%	Tokushima	0.32%
Tokyo	22.03%	Kagawa	0.52%
Kanagawa	9.49%	Ehime	0.54%
Niigata	0.79%	Kochi	0.32%
Toyama	0.59%	Fukuoka	2.74%
Ishikawa	0.66%	Saga	0.27%
Fukui	0.39%	Nagasaki	0.47%
Yamanashi	0.41%	Kumamoto	0.60%
Nagano	1.05%	Oita	0.49%
Gifu	1.17%	Miyazaki	0.41%
Shizuoka	1.99%	Kagoshima	0.56%
Aichi	5.27%	Okinawa	0.70%
Mie	0.94%	Overseas	0.46%

Valid response, 20,000

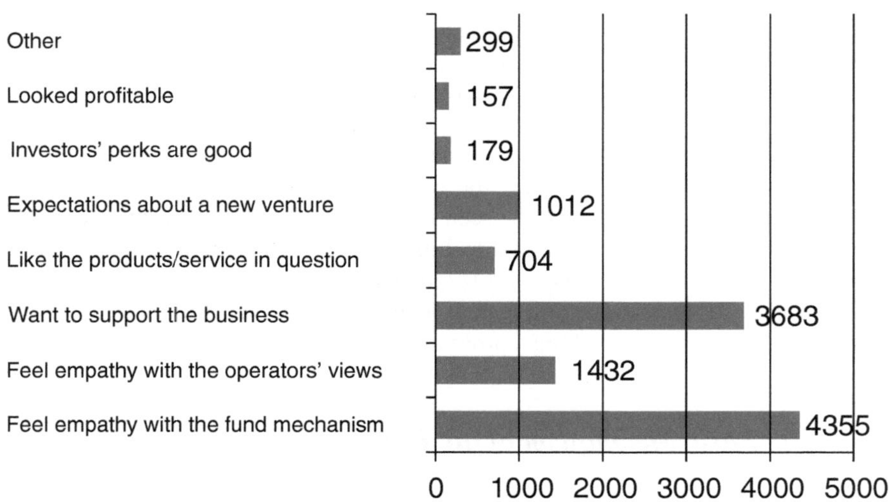

Fig. 3.1 The motives for investing

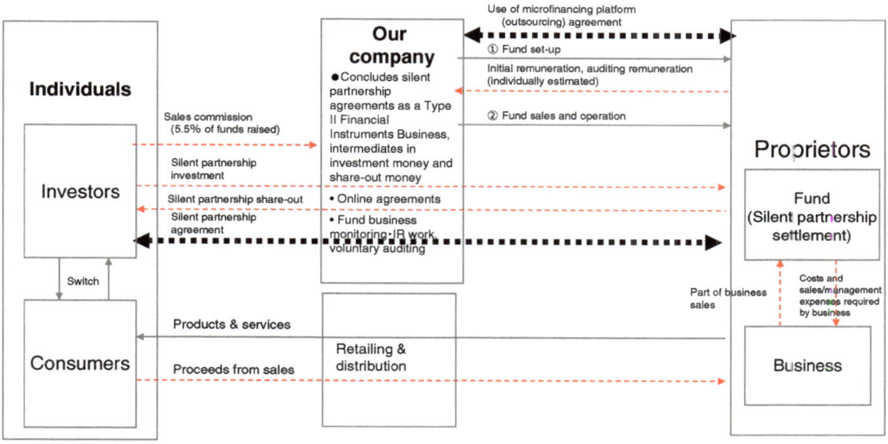

Fig. 3.2 Mechanism of the funds

the proprietors; and as the fund set-up business, creates share-out simulations for the enterprise and the documentation pertaining to silent partnerships. At this stage, our certified public accountants carry out due diligence on the proprietors from the perspective of empathy and feasibility, using information gained from materials related to their management (previous accounts, loans certificates and business plans and so on), visits to their offices and factories, and interviews with the proprietors and other stakeholders. In addition, the concrete business of setting up the fund is pursued after checking to see whether there are any points to empathize with in the proprietors or their business that will entice investors, if the business will be viable throughout the duration of the fund, and if the risks are explainable to investors.

At the stage when offers for the fund are launched, the mediation for the silent partnership agreements and the stakes and dividends is conducted. Furthermore, the monitoring of the business conducted with the silent partnership investment and its IR business, and the voluntary surveillance work of our directorial certified public accountants is conducted.

The agreements are always between the individual investors and the proprietors of the business, and are vis-à-vis agreements between the two parties. The special feature here is that the investor can at the same time be the consumer. Subsequently, the investor is also the purchaser of the product and can be expected to work effectively in a marketing sense as the source of word-of-mouth information about it.

Using our company's IR system, throughout the term of the fund agreement each of the investors is provided with a dedicated webpage where they can log in and check, at any time, the state of the business in which they have invested, and the interest yield. When the term of redemption is reached, the proprietors transfer the funds to our company, and we then distribute these among all the investors, at which point the fund is redeemed.

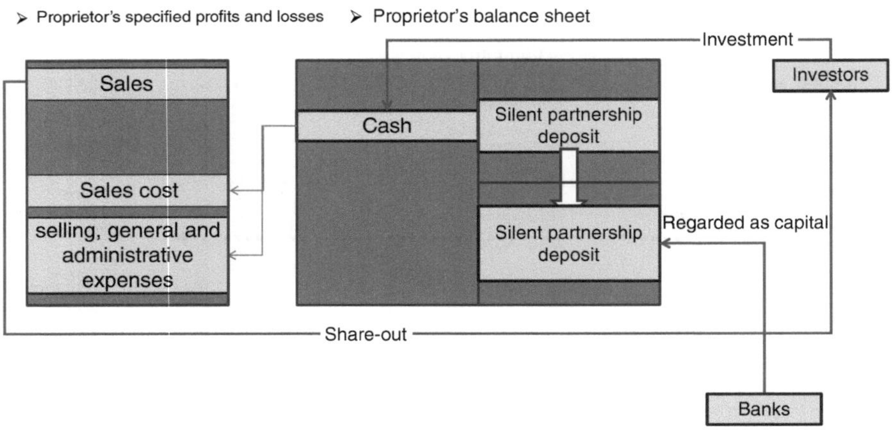

Fig. 3.3 The flow of funds from investment to redemption

Figure 3.3 shows the mechanism from the point of view of the proprietors, who are the recipients. The funds from the investors are placed in the funds section of the balance sheet as cash and received as silent partnership deposits in the debt section. On November 22, 2011, the Financial Services Agency announced a provision with regard to "loans which have sufficient capital capacity (equity loans)" in which it stated that it was permissible to regard these as "capital." It became possible for the banks, under certain conditions, to regard deposits of silent partnerships as capital, enabling the evaluation of financing and making it easier. Subsequently, there are now hopes for improving the balance sheets of companies facing capital shortages and consequent improvements in their management. I think that the Financial Services Agency has made a dramatic improvement to the system in order to revitalize local economies and assist the recovery of disaster areas.

However, since it is the individual financial institutions that actually regard these debts as capital and conduct the financing, progress ends up depending on the business plans and fiscal circumstances of each business receiving financing, and the financing is therefore not actually making much headway. Our company is undergoing detailed discussions with financial institutions in each part of the country, and by persuading as many investors as possible to provide capital we have been able to secure the necessary funding. Furthermore, we are attempting to push through financing by asserting that customers will increase to a higher level than before the investment and that the achievability of business plans will be improved.

In addition, as a new collaboration with these sorts of local financial institutions, an initiative is being launched to promote over-the-counter fund sales at their branches. Since this has been partially successful in the provision of capitalized funds for the recent disaster-hit businesses, we have high hopes for the nationwide use of this mechanism and for an expansion in the amount of money that can be provided. We believe that the key factor here will be the launch of over-the-counter sales of the funds at nearby local financial institutions, where people in the 50s and

Table 3.5 Junmaisyu funds (case of the Oku Harima Fund)

Investment	Fund usage (brewing)	Sales margin	Redemption
Around 3 months	2 years	1 year	2 months
• Fund amount: 6.6 million yen	• Used to cover cost of buying brewer's rice	• After maturing, share-out paid to investors according to amount of sales over 1 year	• After the end of the accounting period the sales results are tabulated and audited within 2 months, and payments transferred to investors' bank accounts
• Amount per single lot (minimum investment): 50,000 yen	• Production of 11,790 bottles (1.8 L size) of junmaisyu sake using brewer's rice		
• Investor perks: approximately eight 720 mL bottles of sake (worth about 9,800 yen)	• Matured for 2 years	• Sales share-out conditions Before recouping: sales × 63.6% After recouping: sales × 1.92% • Share-out simulation Sales of 5.25 million yen: 51% Sales of 10.38 million yen: 100% Sales of 28.32 million: 106%	• Sales results: sales of 33.58 million yen • Yield: 107.2% • Share-out amount: 53,637 yen (before tax)

60s age groups—the groups that have the most financial assets—will be able to buy the products in familiar and safe surroundings. As of October 2012, the company is involved in ongoing collaborative negotiations with 11 local financial institutions regarding such sales.

Table 3.5 shows the flow of funds from the time of investment to redemption, using as an example our Oku Harima Fund, a *junmaisyu* sake fund set up in 2008.

The period of receipt for investments is roughly 3 months, and in the case of this example the total to be raised by the fund was 6.6 million yen with a single-lot investment price (minimum investment price) of 50,000 yen. The per-lot perk for investors was around eight 720 mL bottles of the *junmaisyu* sake, with a retail value of 9,800 yen.

The fund usage period (brewing) was a term of 2 years, with the fund being used for the purchase of brewer's rice. A total of 11,790 bottles (1.8-L size) of the sake were brewed using the brewer's rice, which were then left to mature for a further 2 years.

With regard to the sales record, the sales period was 1 year. After maturation, the payments were shared out among the investors according to the total sales amount of the product over the subsequent year. The sales share-out conditions were 63.6% of sales prior to recouping (the turning point of profit or loss from the point of view of the investors) and 1.92% of sales after recouping. As the share out to investors became less after recouping, the proprietors of the Oku Harima Fund were able to obtain a substantial part of the profits.

Under the share-out simulations, if sales were 5.25 million yen the investors' redemption percentage would be 51%, if the sales were 10.38 million the redemption percentage would be 100%, and if sales were 28.32 million yen the percentage would be 106%. In the event of the redemption share out being 106%, an investor who had invested 50,000 yen would receive a share out of 53,000 yen before tax.

Finally, with regard to redemptions, within 2 months of the end of the accounting period the sales results are tabulated and audited, and the transfer of the sums due to investors begins. In the case of this fund, the sales results reached 33.58 million yen with an earnings yield of 107.2%, and the share-out total was 53,637 yen (before tax) per lot.

1.4 Differences Easily Confused with Other Financial Schemes

Table 3.6 is a comparison of the differences between our fund and other financial schemes with which it is easily confused. The last line of the table cannot strictly be called a financial scheme but is easily confused with one (for reference).

2 Four Cases: Music, Sake, Towels and Forestry

2.1 Case 1: Music Fund

I would like to cite the case of Hip hop Legend 6 (HHL6) as an example of our music fund. This artist is a rapper called AK-69, one of the most celebrated hip hop performers in Japan, and the total amount to be raised was 77.39 million yen with a single lot retailing at 10,000 yen. The accounting period of the fund started on January 26, 2011 and was redeemed on September 25 that year. The redemption result was 104.84%.

AK-69 sold 8,090 copies of his Paint the World album, which was released in 2004, and the amount to be raised by the fund was 12 million yen. The total amount of the recent HHL6 fund was 77.39 million yen, and the 2011 album created using the fund, entitled The Red Magic, sold 100,488 copies. It reached third in the Oricon charts and became a massive hit.

AK-69 has used 14 of our music funds over the past 8 years, with a total fund amount of 333 million yen, an average yield of 111.3% and a plus yield of 11.3%. Whilst sticking to his independent music activities he has received two consecutive Golden Album awards from the Recording Industry Association of Japan in recognition of selling over 100,000 copies of an album, something that is difficult to

Table 3.6 Comparison of the differences between our fund and other financial schemes

	Fund providers	Fund recipients	Funding method	Redemption/exit	Monetary return	Regulations[a]	Scheme management qualification[b]	Receipt method
Microfinancing schemes	Individuals (small lot)	Mainly small-to-medium-size enterprises	Investment in business (investment with no acquisition of shares)	Percentage of sales shared out as decided at time of agreement	Decided upon according to sales of investment project at time of redemption	Financial instruments and exchange act	Type II financial instruments business operators	Received as silent partnerships deposit in balance sheet's liabilities section. Regarded as capital under certain conditions
Micro credit scheme known as "microfi-nancing"	Monetary and financial institutions (MFI)[b]	Individuals,small-scale businesses (small lot)	Finance	Principal plus loan interest returned	Decided upon beforehand as loan interest	Money lending control act	Money lending	Debt in the case of individuals, leverage on balance sheet in the case of corporations
Venture capital/ private equity funds	Investment partnerships	Venture businesses, limited companies in general	Investment through acquisition of shares	Stock market listings and buyouts through mergers and acquisitions	Capital gain at the time of stock sale	None under certain conditions of the financial instruments and exchange act	None under certain conditions	Capital funds through allocation of new shares to a third party, received as capital reserve
Scheme known as "crowd funding"	Individuals (small lot)	Individuals, small-scale businesses (small lot)	Donations, prior purchase of goods or services	None	None	None	None	Usually, as well as donations and prior purchases, funds allocated as sales (ordinary revenue) received

[a]The Japanese case is hypothetical here, though results may vary from country to country
[b]The terms are explained in Chap. 4

achieve even for artists on major record labels. He has become the foremost hip-hop artist in Japan using music funds.

2.2 *Case 2: Junmaisyu Sake Fund*

The purpose of the Junmaisyu Fund is to support breweries aiming to make *junmaisyu* sake created entirely from pure rice, and their efforts to continue making sake that is matured for 3 years.

The issues that the breweries face are the difficulty of obtaining loans for more than a year from banks, the harsh reality that they cannot make any profits from their own funds during the 3 years during which the sake is maturing, and the high price of their raw materials.

The Junmaisyu Fund is the measure taken to resolve these difficulties. It enables the setting up of funds worth several million yen to cover raw materials during each season; comparatively long-term loans of 3–5 years are available; the sake lovers who invest in the funds are able to enjoy the changing taste of the sake as it matures, and the breweries themselves are be able to put their product on sale on a schedule with which they are satisfied.

The brewery in the Oku Harima Fund I explained above was the Shimomura Brewery, an old company founded in Hyogo Prefecture in western Japan in the year 1884. The amount to be raised by the fund was 6.6 million yen, and lots could be purchased at a price of 10,000 yen each. The accounting period of the fund started on January 1, 2009, and the fund was redeemed on December 31, 2011, with a redemption result of 107.27%.

Starting with the fund for the Shinkame Brewery in Saitama Prefecture we have set up 19 Junmaisyu Funds in all, with a total value of 226.75 million yen. All this money has been devoted to the purchase from farmers of brewer's rice.

The Junmaisyu Fund empathizes with the brewers' strict ideals for *junmaisyu*, and their fierce insistence that all the sake made at their brewery be *junmaisyu*. The perks for investors include being sent eight 720 mL bottles of the *junmaisyu* sake (though the amount differs from one fund to another) and invitations to see the sake being produced at the brewery, both of which have increased empathy among the investors. Moreover, providing the share out by 'payment in kind' raises great expectations as a form of non-monetary returns. All the investors are also delighted with the limited edition sake cups sent to them (Fig. 3.4) as proof of their investment.

As a result of the use of the Junmaisyu Fund, the sales of the Shimomura Brewery were mostly flat from 2008 to 2010, but the matured sake produced with the money from the 2008 Oku Harima Fund went on sale in 2011 and by June 2011 sales had increased by 108% on the previous term, and by 116% on the previous term by June 2012. Shimomura Brewery has used four Junmaisyu funds, in the years 2008, 2009, 2011 and 2012. Only able to borrow from the banks for the short period of 1 year, they had been unable to produce the matured sake that makes the most of the local

Fig. 3.4 The limited edition sake cups

rice in the area—rice that is particularly suited to sake production—but they were able to use the funds to procure loans payable over the long term, and develop their business in a manner that could maximize their regional resources. The money "waiting" in the fund became the resource for creating a mature type of sake that is slightly more expensive than non-matured sake, and turned into the catalyst behind raising the added value of the brewery.

2.3 *Case 3: Towel Fund*

The purpose of the towel fund can be stated as follows: expanding the use of organic cotton towels—which currently account for less than 1% of the world towel market—and providing educational activities will improve the quality of life of the Tanzanian farmers who produce the organic cotton, and expand sales by commercialising new products.

The issues that had to be faced were that the towel manufacturer had undergone civil rehabilitation proceedings in the past and therefore found it difficult to raise funds, and how to raise the product's public recognition and expand its fan base.

The significance of the towel fund is that it boosts the consumption of organic cotton instead of the usual cotton, which consumes the most agrochemicals, and provides ongoing support through private investment for the new initiative of "factory brands" from Imabari City in Ehime Prefecture.

The target for the "Wind-Weave Towel Fund" was Ikeuchi Towel Co., Ltd., which purchases organic cotton produced in Tanzania and manufactures the "Cotton Nouveau" range. The amount to be raised by the fund was 5.5 million yen, and a single lot is 50,000 yen. The accounting period of the fund started on April 1, 2011, and was redeemed on March 31, 2012. The redemption result was a positive redemption of 104.18%.

Subscriptions for the fund were first launched in 2010 and the cotton towel project made a new start with the fund in 2011. The towels proved to be a popular product—they were completely sold out from the first year, and in the second year the company was flooded with bookings for the product before they went on sale. Sales expanded further after the towels were featured on the TV Tokyo program "Cambria Palace" and the Wind-Weave towels were adopted as goods for the official shop of the Tokyo Skytree, a broadcasting tower that is the tallest building in Japan.

The fund was used for each year's series in both 2011 and 2012, and a new project with a powerful message was achieved through the fund. It proved to be a precious route for raising funds from core fans, and was able to boost the company's business activities.

2.4 Case 4: Forestry Fund

The purpose of the forestry fund is to leave forests for future generations and revitalize the forestry business.

The issues faced by foresters were that trees that ought to be profitable were being left untended, no progress was being made in introducing forestry machinery and costs were high, and there was a low level of awareness and interest about the merits and value of using domestically produced wood.

The solution to these issues is the forestry fund. Through investment, the fund increases opportunities for people to become interested in domestically produced wood, the raising of funds helps to purchase forestry equipment and bring down costs, and there are more opportunities for profit due to the effective use of domestically produced timber from forest thinning.

The target of the "Nishiawakura Village Joint Forestry Fund 2009" was a company called Tobimushi Inc. The company purchased forestry machinery using money from the fund. The amount to be raised by the fund was 49.40 million yen, and the price advertised for a single lot was 50,000 yen. The accounting period of the fund, which is still ongoing, started on July 1, 2009, and the redemption date is scheduled for June 30, 2019.

The empathy points of this fund are that you cannot have a good forest unless it is managed properly, that forestry can put to use some precious resources that are now lying dormant in Japan, and that local tours can spark friendships and strengthen links between companies. The photographs in Fig. 3.5 show the sort of forest that is desirable, not the cramped and thin trees to the left but woods like the one to the right where light can penetrate and the trees grow with thick, healthy trunks.

Subscriptions for the fund were launched in 2009, and the fund was used to purchase forestry machinery. Nishiawakura Forest School Limited, a subsidiary of Tobimushi Inc. that serves as a trading house for the forestry products, became the only private sector company in Okayama Prefecture's Nishiawakura Village to

Fig. 3.5 Nishiawakura forest

generate sales of over 100 million yen in 2011. This also led to the creation of employment, and it became the only village in the entire prefecture where the population is actually increasing.

With the drawing together of over 400 investors from across Japan (including those of the "Nishiawakura Village Joint Forestry Fund 2010"), not only was it possible to buy forestry machinery but it engendered expectations from around the nation, thus raising the local people's enthusiasm. The fund investors are becoming publicity agents for Nishiawakura Village, and contributing to the increase of income in the village by, for example, regularly purchasing rice from local farmers.

3 Five Cases for Recovery: The "Securité Disaster Area Support Fund"

3.1 Outline and Basic Mechanism

I will now explain the Securité Disaster Area Support Fund as an example of a fund's use in the field of earthquake disaster relief.

The Securité Disaster Area Support Fund was used by 37 companies to set up 38 funds in four prefectures from Hokkaido to Fukushima, which were hit by the earthquake disaster of March 11, 2011. The total amount to be raised by the fund was 1.1 billion yen, of which approximately 900 million yen has been realized as of October 2012.

As illustrated in Fig. 3.6 the basic mechanism of the fund is similar to the other silent partnership investment funds. However, the unique characteristic of the Securité Disaster Area Support Fund is that the single lots of 10,000 yen are split into a 5,000-yen investment and a 5,000-yen charitable donation, with half of the amount being provided as a donation for which no return is necessary. Some examples of the main activities that the fund has actually enabled are described below.

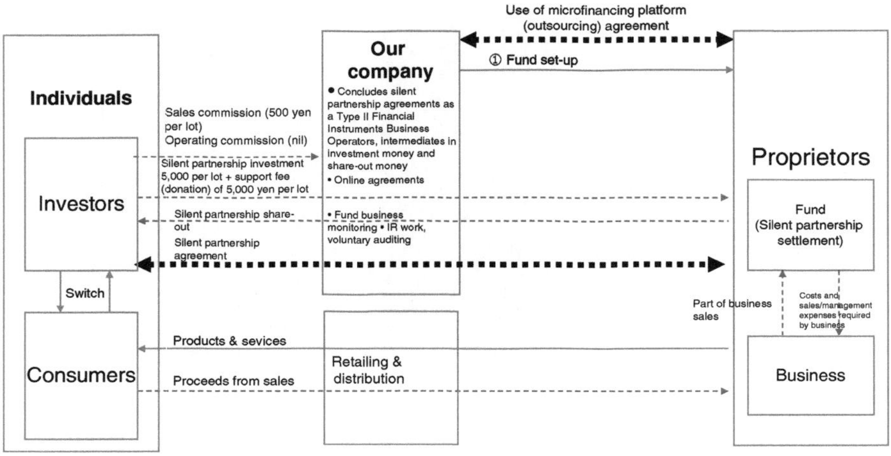

Fig. 3.6 Examples of the main activities that the fund has enabled

3.1.1 Case 5: Yamauchi Fish Traders Fund

The target of the fund was the owner of Yamauchi Fish Traders who is also the chair of the planning committee in charge of driving the restoration and recovery of Minami Sanriku Town. The fund raised a total of 50 million yen among 1,454 investors, started on July 1, 2011 and is scheduled for redemption on December 31, 2020. The funds were used to purchase processing equipment such as the machinery shown in Fig. 3.7.

The funds were raised between the months of May and September 2011. A temporary factory was constructed in another part of Minami Sanriku Town and equipment was purchased using the funds, with the factory restarting from June 2012.

3.1.2 Case 6: Saikichi Trading Fund

With an objective of "taking this opportunity to make our products at least better than before the earthquake" the company purchased various equipment as shown in Fig. 3.8. The amount raised by the fund was 10 million yen among 400 investors. It started on August 1, 2012 and is scheduled for redemption on March 31, 2018.

The funds were raised between April and May 2011, with equipment being purchased with the funds and the company's factory restarting in July 2012.

3.1.3 Case 7: Ishiwatari Trading Shark Fin Fund

With the objective of restoring Kesennuma City's reputation as the town of shark fins, funds of 100 million yen were raised among 2,532 investors. The fund started

Fig. 3.7 Machinery of Yamauchi Fish Traders at Minami Sanriku Town purchased by using the fund

Fig. 3.8 Sakichi Trading

on September 1, 2012, and it is expected that it will be redeemed on December 31, 2019. The company used the funds to purchase equipment for its new factory, which restarted operations in August 2012.

Since there was a particularly large number of investors for the Ishiwatari Trading Shark Fin Fund, 2,532 in all, there are high hopes that these investors will also become consumers of the company's products.

3.1.4 Case 8: Tsuda Fish Traders Fund

Tsuda Fish Traders operates as an "evolving fish trader" in the city of Ishimaki, its activities including the sales of fish to stores and the development of its online sales and joint management of restaurants. The value of the fund was 15 million yen, and comprised 590 investors. It started on March 1, 2012 and is scheduled for redemption on May 31, 2019. The funds were used to make improvements to and equip stores, which reopened in February 2012.

3.1.5 Case 9: Tatsumi Foods Seaweed Fund

Located in Ishimaki City, Tatsumi Foods is the pioneering company that turned the city's Jusanhama beach area into a seaweed production centre. The fund raised 10 million yen among 431 investors. The fund was launched on May 1, 2012 and is scheduled for redemption on April 30, 2022. The funds were used to develop a factory, which went into operation on the site where the old factory was located in April 2012.

References

United Nations Centre for Regional Development (UNCRD) (2012) Case study on reconstruction towards sustainable communities in Tohoku area. UNCRD, Nagoya, p 4. http://www.uncrd.or.jp/events/doc/[Iwate]%20Case%20Study%20on%20Reconstruction%20towards%20Sustainable%20Communities%20in%20Tohoku%20Area.pdf. Accessed 31 Oct 2012

World Bank (2011) Knowledge note 4–5, cluster 4 recovery planning, livelihood and job creation. World Bank, p 15. http://wbi.worldbank.org/wbi/Data/wbi/wbicms/files/drupal-acquia/wbi/drm_kn4-5_0.pdf. Accessed 31 Oct 2012

Chapter 4
Hometown Investment Trust Funds for Regional Development

Norifumi Sugimoto

1 Overview

Chapter 2 summarises the characteristics of Hometown Investment Trust (HIT) as follows.

- Small financial instruments that do not go through a financial institution's balance sheets.
- A new fund-sharing channel that utilizes "individuals' goodwill" and "characteristics of risk tolerance that differs from that of financial institutions".
- Consideration given to the independence of investment destination business operators in accordance with the mode of investment in silent relationships.
- Direct participation by individual investors through transactions via the Internet.
- Through large numbers of individual investors continuing to be involved through investment, they are converted into consumers (fans) who support the said business.

Based on these perspectives, this chapter considers two fields which hold even greater promise for the utilization of HIT schemes.

Specifically, this refers to the utilization of HIT schemes related to (1) "regional development that utilizes local industry and attracts new business start-ups" as part of earthquake disaster reconstruction, and (2) the Kokusyu (Sake and Shochu) Project, which government bodies are promoting cooperatively from the perspective of "locally generated global marketing."

N. Sugimoto (✉)
Regional Planning Department, Development Bank of Japan Inc., Tokyo, Japan
e-mail: norifumi.sugimoto@gmail.com

N. Yoshino and S. Kaji (eds.), *Hometown Investment Trust Funds: A Stable Way to Supply Risk Capital*, DOI 10.1007/978-4-431-54309-1_4, © Springer Japan 2013

2 The Case of Ishinomaki

2.1 Overview of Public Finance Responses to the Great East Japan Earthquake

The Great East Japan Earthquake wrought immense damage, leaving more than 18,000 people either dead or missing and more than 6,000 injured, with nearly 400,000 buildings wholly or partially destroyed. The disaster zone is gradually moving from the actual restoration stage to the reconstruction stage, but there are still some 340,000 people forced to live in temporary housing. In order to halt the population outflow from the disaster zone, urgent "regional reconstruction development" is required (Murate 2012).

2.1.1 Public Finance Responses

Focusing on public finance aspects, government reconstruction support measures such as the First Supplementary Budget approved in May 2011 allocated four trillion yen for disposing disaster waste, restoring public infrastructure, and constructing temporary housing, etc. The Second Supplementary Budget approved in July allocated two trillion yen to support disaster survivors, among others.

The Third Supplementary Budget—which became a full-blown reconstruction budget—secured financial resources through the issue of reconstruction bonds, etc., and allocated 9.2438 trillion yen for reconstruction-related expenditures, including allowances for

1. Great East Japan Reconstruction Grants established under the Special Recovery Area Act (1.5612 trillion yen)
2. Additional public works, etc. (1.4734 trillion yen)
3. Expenditures for nationwide disaster prevention measures (575.2 billion yen)
4. Expenditures for disaster-related financial loans (671.6 billion yen)

Moreover, a so-called Group Subsidy System (Program for Subsidising the Restoration of Facilities Shared by Small and Medium-sized Company Associations) aimed at shopping districts, which are indispensable for local communities, and basic local industries and clusters is being implemented. Under this system, groups of small and medium-sized enterprises (SME) forming the "core of the local economy" can take the lead in reconstruction, formulate and submit reconstruction project plans, and can receive subsidies for the restoration and/or repair of facilities and equipment if their application is approved by the prefectural government. For SMEs, subsidies cover three-fourths of the cost (one-half of which is covered by the national government and one-quarter by the prefectural government) and for large enterprises subsidies cover one-half of the cost (one-third of which by the national government and one-sixth by the prefectural government). This system is regarded as effective in the restoration and restructuring of local industry, and thus far a total of 290.7 billion yen in subsidies has been granted to 338 projects (as of May 2012). However, because under the present system the documentation required for subsidy application requires a substantial number of hours and is a burden for system users, the scale of total subsidy amounts is limited and further improvement of the system is desired (Murate 2012).

2.2 *Overview of Financial Responses to the Great East Japan Earthquake*

2.2.1 Financial Responses by the Public Sector

With regard to financial aspects, responses to the so-called overlapping debt problem as well as a Special Recovery Area Interest Subsidy System and emergency response financial loans, etc., are also being implemented.

Below is an initial overview of government responses (Table 4.1).

Industrial Reconstruction Organisations

With regard to the problem of so-called overlapping debt, in which existing debt becomes a burden making the procurement of new loans difficult, in June 2011, "Policies Regarding Countermeasures to the Overlapping Debt Problem" were decided at a relevant ministerial conference. These policies included countermeasures "for SMEs and the agriculture/forestry/fisheries industries," "for personal housing loans," and "for financial institutions."

Based on these policies, the government established "industrial reconstruction organizations" as sources of revitalisation funds to inject capital into SMEs with the potential for turnaround but which have excessive debt, as well as to provide assistance for the purchase of non-performing loans. Limited partnerships for investment were to be established in each prefecture, with the Organization for Small and Medium-sized Enterprises and Regional Innovation and financial institutions providing capital injection.

As of March 2012, industrial reconstruction organisations have been established in Iwate, Miyagi, Fukushima, and Ibaraki prefectures, and as of September 2012, the purchase of non-performing loans in a total of 31 cases (16 in Iwate Prefecture, 12 in Miyagi Prefecture, 2 in Fukushima Prefecture, and 1 in Ibaraki Prefecture) have been decided (website of industrial reconstruction organizations).

Turnaround Initiative Corporation for Business Operators in the Area of the Great East Japan Earthquake

In addition, in the National Diet, while reform initiatives by the Liberal Democratic Party, New Komeito, the Sunrise Party of Japan, and Japan New Party have gradually lessened the burden of debt on eligible business operators, it was also decided

Table. 4.1 Public finance measures aimed at reconstruction (as of September 2012)

	Industrial reconstruction organizations (Already established in Iwate, Miyagi, Fukushima, Ibaraki, and Chiba Prefectures)	Turnaround initiative corporation for business operators in the area of the Great East Japan Earthquake	Small and medium enterprise turnaround support committee
Form of organization	Limited partnership for investment	Limited company	Chamber of commerce and industry, prefectural federations of societies of commerce and industry, one division of the prefectural industrial development corporation
Date of establishment	Iwate: November 11, 2011 Ibaraki: November 30, 2011 Miyagi: December 22, 2011 Fukushima: December 27, 2011 Chiba: March 28, 2012	February 22, 2012 (date of application for organizing registration)	Established one-by-one beginning in February 2003
Purpose of establishment	• Provide support, including capital injection, loan purchasing, and DES (Dead Equity Swap) for small and medium enterprises whose business can be turned around but that have excessive debt • Identify the needs of enterprises in the disaster zone for short-term turnaround schemes and consider support by the Enterprise Turnaround Initiative Corporation of Japan ("Policies Regarding Countermeasures to the Overlapping Debt Problem" approved by the Cabinet on June 17, 2011)	• To sustain economic activity in the Great East Japan Earthquake disaster zone by preventing the outflow of industry and people from the disaster zone to other regions and accordingly, through collaboration with financial institutions and local public organizations, lessening the burden of debt and supporting the turnaround of business owners bearing excessive debt due to damage caused by the Great East Japan earthquake who are attempting to rebuilt their business in the disaster zone through financial institutions, etc., purchasing the debts of the said business owners and other activities in order to support reconstruction in the disaster zone. (Article 1 of the Turnaround Initiative Corporation for Business Operators in the Area of the Great East Japan Earthquake Act)	• To conduct detailed survey analyses of enterprises' business activities and finances from the fair and impartial standpoint of a third party, and to support turnaround plan proposals by debtors after conducting an analysis of the cause of an enterprise's difficulties as well as submitting turnaround proposals to financial institutions and implementing financial institution reconciliation. (Website of the Small and Medium Enterprise Turnaround Support Committee)

Contri-butory	Organization for Small and Medium Enterprises and Regional Innovation: 80 % Prefecture or financial institutions with the relevant prefecture: 20 %	National government: 20 billion yen	(Project commissioned by the national government)
Eligible entities	• Business owners whose companies can be reestablished but who are burdened with excessive debt due to the disaster and who are attempting to rebuild their business within the disaster zone (Excludes large enterprises)	• Business owners who are burdened with excessive debt due to the disaster and who are attempting to rebuild their business within the disaster zone • Includes small business owners, agriculture/forestry/fisheries business owners, health/welfare business owners, etc. (Excludes large enterprises and third-sector enterprises)	SMEs
Period for deciding support (investment period)	Iwate: 2 years 2 months (may be extended by 1 year) Miyagi: 2 years (may be extended by 1 year) Fukushima: 3 years (may be extended by 1 year) Ibaraki: 2 years (may be extended) Chiba: 2 years (may be extended by 1 year)	• Within 5 years of the date of establishment (1-year extension possible with ministerial approval)	No time limitation (regulations requiring review before March 31, 2016 under the Act on Special Measures concerning Industrial Revitalization)
Support period	12 years (may be extended for 3 years) (Period of existence of the organization)	Within 15 years, as a general rule	[Period of turnaround plan] • Rescheduling: within 20 years, as a general rule • Debt forgiving, etc.: 3–5 years
Main activities	• Purchase of claims (loans, capital injection, etc.)	• Purchase of claims • Loans (limited to bridging finance) • Debt guarantees • Capital injection • Dispatch of experts • Advice on business activities	• Support in formulating turnaround plans • Creditor reconciliation

(continued)

Table. 4.1 (continued)

	Industrial reconstruction organizations (Already established in Iwate, Miyagi, Fukushima, Ibaraki, and Chiba Prefectures)	Turnaround initiative corporation for business operators in the area of the Great East Japan Earthquake	Small and medium enterprise turnaround support committee
Performance	Iwate 2011: 6 purchases 2012: 10 purchases Miyagi 2011: 5 purchases 2012: 7 purchases Fukushima 2012: 2 purchases Ibaraki 2012: 1 purchase Chiba 2012: 1 purchase	2012: Support decided in 19 cases	2011 (including cases not related to the earthquake disaster) 1,741 consultations 255 turnaround plans formulated
Disclosure of supported enterprises	Undisclosed	Undisclosed	Undisclosed

to establish the Turnaround Initiative Corporation for Business Operators in the Area of the Great East Japan Earthquake (http://www.etic-j.co.jp/) with the purpose of providing support for business revitalisation.

The Turnaround Initiative Corporation for Business Operators in the Area of the Great East Japan Earthquake was established on February 22, 2012, with a head office located in the city of Sendai and Tokyo headquarters located in Tokyo, as well as prefectural industrial reconstruction consultation centres providing consultation services across-the-board. As of July 27, 2012, assistance has been granted to ten applicants. In the future, when business operators in the disaster zone are considering full-scale renewal or beginning new operations, many of these operators will need to reduce the burden of existing loans first. Thus it was decided to shorten the time taken for the Turnaround Initiative Corporation to approve applications for assistance (the usual 180-day (approximate) period for handling cases was reduced to around 90 days and shortened even further for small business operators). In addition, the Reconstruction Agency, Financial Services Agency, and Small and Medium-sized Enterprise Agency were to cooperate in preparing promotional packages and provide support for the Turnaround Initiative Corporation in its endeavours (http://www.shien-kiko.co.jp/).

Small and Medium-Sized Enterprise Turnaround Support Committee

In the Second Supplementary Budget for 2012, the Small and Medium-sized Enterprise Turnaround Support Committee was allocated three billion yen for a Structural Strengthening of the Small and Medium-sized Enterprise Turnaround Support Committee under the heading "Expenditure Related to Support for Disaster Victims," and measures aimed at reconstruction are being taken (http://www.meti.go.jp/english/press/2012/0321_02.html).

Special Reconstruction District Interest Subsidy System

A Special Reconstruction District Interest Subsidy System has also been established. Under this system, when financial institutions designated in accordance with the Act on Special Districts for Reconstruction from the Great East Japan Earthquake provide loans to core businesses that have fulfilled the aims of the reconstruction promotion plan (plans decided by specified local public organisations in the disaster zone and approved by the national government), they receive an interest subsidy from the national government for the said loans (maximum of 0.7 % for a maximum term of 5 years). Businesses in nine stipulated fields are eligible, including healthcare-related businesses, agriculture/forestry/fisheries industry-related businesses, energy-related businesses, businesses that enhance and invigorate local industry (create employment opportunities) (Hasue 2012).

Crisis Response Loans

In the First Supplementary Budget announced in May 2011, the Japan Finance Corporation was allocated 2.5 trillion yen for crisis response activities (aimed at medium-sized and large enterprises). In the Third Supplementary Budget announced in November 2011, an additional 1.5 trillion yen was allocated to these crisis response activities, and a further 2.0 trillion yen was allocated in the 2012 Budget (Development Bank of Japan 2012).

2.2.2 Financial Responses by the Private Sector

As described above, the Japanese government is implementing various financial reconstruction support measures, while the private sector is also establishing funds for reconstruction.

Funds for reconstruction can be roughly divided into (1) aid-type, (2) investment-type, and (3) loan-type funds (Table 4.2).

Looking at the targeted recipients of support, in addition to target enterprises having distinctive features with regard to scale (large and small), these funds mainly target enterprises in industrial or public works fields.

Specifically, aid-type and investment-type funds can be subdivided into "living infrastructure," "operational activities," and "social business" funds.

Furthermore, looking at the fields receiving support, reconstruction funds—including "social community business-type," "new venture-generating-type," "regional development-type," and "business turnaround-type" funds—are being established in response to funding needs.

There are also funds being establishing in collaboration with local financial institutions in the disaster zone (websites of various private-sector funds) (Fig. 4.1).

2.3 Characteristics and Performance of HIT: From the Perspective of Regional Reconstruction Development

The previous sections provide an overview of public finance and financial aspects as well as public and private reconstruction support measures. However, in circumstances where regional reconstruction development needs to be gaining momentum, there is undoubtedly need for further strengthening of the framework for such support from a broader perspective.

Regional development issues that must be overcome are the resurrection of (1) safe and secure towns that protect residents from tsunami; (2) towns with neighbourhoods that can sustain communities; and (3) towns with "places to work" which are the foundation for people's everyday living.

Many areas in the disaster zone have been suffering from population decreases since before the disaster. Many businesses in central city districts have been shut

Table 4.2 Overview of reconstruction funds

Name of fund	Main contributory/defrayer	Overview
Loan-type/investment-type (Debt/Mezzanine/Equity)		
Miyagi Support Fund	The Sendai Bank, Ltd.	Loan fund aimed at reconstruction in the disaster zone (total amount: 20 billion yen)
Business Reconstruction Assistance Fund	Mizuho Bank, Ltd.	Loan fund aimed at businesses damaged by the earthquake disaster/harmful rumors (total amount: 200 billion yen)
Sanriku Recovery Friends Fund	Kesennuma Shinkin Bank and others	Interest subsidy fund for SMEs in coastal areas. Joint investment by US NGO Mercy Corps and the Kesennuma Shinkin Bank. Operated by NPO Planet Finance Japan (total amount: two million US dollars)
Iwate Genki-ippai Limited Partnership for Investment	The Bank of Iwate, Ltd; Development Bank of Japan, Inc.	Mezzanine fund aimed at reconstruction in the disaster zone (compositional amount: five billion yen)
Fukushima Support Fund Limited Partnership for Investment	The Toho Bank, Ltd.; Development Bank of Japan, Inc.	Mezzanine fund aimed at reconstruction in the disaster zone (compositional amount: five billion yen)
Miyagi Reconstruction Bridge Limited Partnership for Investment	The 77 Bank, Ltd.; Development Bank of Japan, Inc.	Mezzanine fund aimed at reconstruction in the disaster zone (compositional amount: five billion yen)
Ibaraki Kizuna Limited Partnership for Investment	The Ibaraki Bank, Ltd; Development Bank of Japan, Inc.	Mezzanine fund aimed at reconstruction in the disaster zone (compositional amount: five billion yen)
Recovery Support Fund "Shinkin-no-kizuna"	Shinkin Central Bank	Mezzanine fund for Shinkin Central Bank trading partners in the three disaster zone prefectures (total amount: five billion yen)
Securité Disaster Area Support Funds	Music Securities, Inc.	Micro fund aimed at reconstruction in the disaster zone targeting investment for the cultivation and turnaround of local industries
Great East Japan Small/Medium Business Reconstruction Support Limited Partnership for Investment	The 77 Bank, Ltd.; Organization for Small & Medium Enterprises and Regional Innovation, Japan; and others	Equity fund aimed at reconstruction in the disaster zone for small/medium businesses (compositional amount: seven billion yen)
Mizuho Tohoku Industry Development Fund	Mizuho Bank, Ltd.; Mizuho Corporate Bank, Ltd.	Equity fund aimed at reconstruction in the disaster zone (compositional amount: six billion yen)

(continued)

Table 4.2 (continued)

Name of fund	Main contributory/defrayer	Overview
Aid-type (resident, enterprise, other)		
Tohoku Common Benefit Investment Fund	UNIQLO Co., Ltd. and others	Fund providing capital injection for public-interest investment and taking on public corporation bonds (total amount of capital injection, etc.: 500 million yen)
Yamato Welfare Foundation	Yamato Transport Co., Ltd.	Provides aid to local public agencies and public-interest corporations providing support for reconstruction of living infrastructure and the revitalization of fisheries and agricultural industries in the disaster zone (target: 30 billion yen). Aid ended after the fifth public offering
Great East Japan Earthquake Recovery Initiatives Foundation	Softbank Corp.	Fund subsidizing funds for children's education and living support in the disaster zone
Coca-Cola Reconstruction Support Fund	The Coca-Cola Company	Fund providing side for public facilities, etc. that are necessary for the rehabilitation of the living conditions of children affected by the disaster, beginning with educational facilities
Qatar Friendship Fund	Government of Qatar	Fund providing donations to businesses and organizations in the fisheries, health, and educational fields in the disaster zone [total amount: eight billion yen (100 million USD)]
MAKOTO	Tomohiro Takei	Fund supporting venture and SMEs in the disaster zone
Mitsubishi Corporation Disaster Relief Foundation	Mitsubishi Corporation	Provides capital injection and aid aimed at supporting the activities of oNPOs, NGOs, and other organizations involved in recovery and reconstruction activities in the disaster zone (total amount: ten billion yen)
Shinrai Zaidan	Donations from residents, etc.	Public interest incorporated foundation aimed at supporting Great East Japan Earthquake Disaster reconstruction (has a system for subsidizing employment costs)
Securité Disaster Area Support Funds	Music Securities, Inc.	Micro fund targeting investment for the cultivation and turnaround of local industries

(continued)

Table 4.2 (continued)

Name of fund	Main contributory/defrayer	Overview
(Investment trust)		
East Japan Revival Support Bond Fund 1105	Nomura Securities Co., Ltd.	Investment trust that mainly takes on the industrial bonds of enterprises located in the disaster zone
Daiwa Nippon Ouen Fund Vol. 3	Daiwa Securities Co. Ltd.	Investment trust that mainly takes on the industrial bonds of enterprises located in the disaster zone
Shinkin Reconstruction Assistance Scholarship Fund	Shinkin banks and their affiliated groups	Investment trust that mainly takes on the public corporation bonds of local government agencies and enterprises in the disaster zone

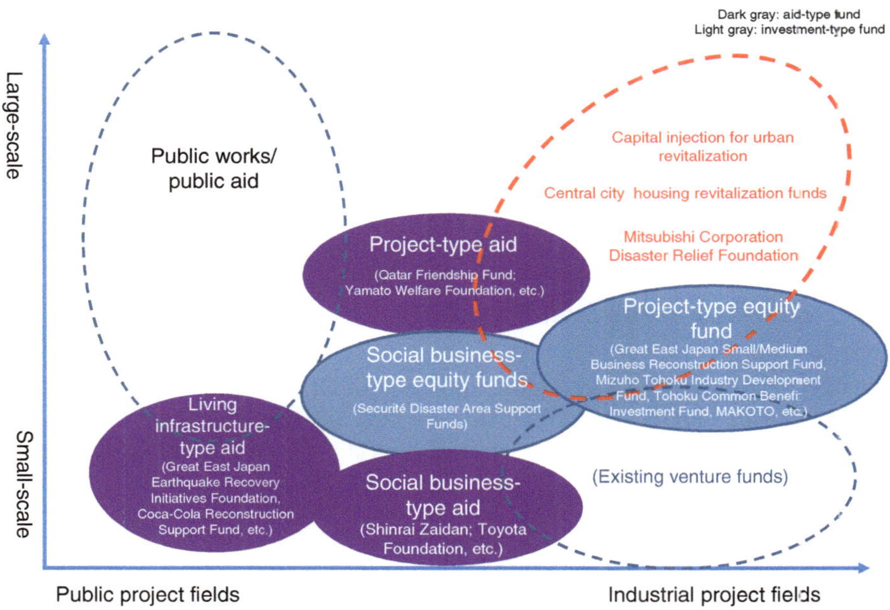

Fig. 4.1 Aid-type/investment-type reconstruction funds

down and the areas have lost their vibrancy and bustle, which further causes residents to move away from these areas—a vicious cycle. In order to transform the quagmire caused by the earthquake into an opportunity and promote attractive and vigorous regional town development, it is imperative that local industries are resurrected, including the establishment of new businesses and not merely the restoration of damaged stores and businesses to their pre-disaster state.

2.3.1 Performance of the Securité Disaster Area Support Fund

To enable this, commensurate risk management is necessary, but HIT schemes can be said to hold the potential for playing a tremendously useful role in regional reconstruction development.

Music Securities, Inc.'s Securité Disaster Area Support Fund[1] is characterized by the functionality and speed with which it assists with the reconstruction of local industries.

The Securité Disaster Area Support Fund functions as a combination of aid-type and investment-type fund—a so-called hybrid fund—and began collecting donations for disaster relief with astonishing speed in April 2011—less than 2 months after the Great East Japan Earthquake. The fund has already established 34 funds providing a total of approximately one billion yen that is being used by 33 business operators. The fund has more than approximately 23,000 contributors, who invest via the Internet, and is gathering "goodwill" funds contributed by people throughout the country out of a desire to assist projects aimed at reconstruction of the disaster zone, rather than receive any returns from the fund.

The scale of individual funds is small, ranging from 7 to 100 million yen (equity), but the speedy handling of applications match the funding needs of small business operators, and commercial/retail stores will play an essential role in future regional reconstruction development, and the fund is receiving high praise from users and investors alike.

Furthermore, based on this performance, according to Music Securities, Inc. Miyagi Prefecture is planning to add the company's fund activities to the prefectural menu of support for disaster zone enterprises (Komatsu 2012).

2.4 Overview of the Ishinomaki Town Reconstruction Project

What is being envisioned for the full utilization of HIT schemes in future regional town reconstruction development? This question is examined below through the example of the central town reconstruction project being carried out in Ishinomaki City, Miyagi Prefecture.

2.4.1 Study Framework for the Ishinomaki Town Reconstruction Project

The Ishinomaki Town Reconstruction Project is being carried out in Ishinomaki's central area as part of a reconstruction/redevelopment concept. In May 2011, an Ishinomaki Reconstruction Council was launched by the local Ishinomaki community with the aim

[1] The name of this fund has so far been translated in more ways than one. The World Bank (2011) called it the "Japan Earthquake Securité Supporting Fund" while the United Nations (2012) refers to it as "Disaster Site Support Fund." Others categorise this fund under the broader name of "Earthquake Relief Fund." The name used in this text is a direct and official translation of the Japanese name, reflecting the name of our company, Music Securities.

of ensuring the realization of this project. A base—the Ishinomaki Community Café—was established in the disaster-stricken central city district. Discussions and information sharing regarding regional reconstruction development took place with Machizukuri Mambo Co. with central town store owners taking a central role, and study meetings with specialists and university personnel as invited participants were actively organized. Amidst these activities, independent urban development review committees were established in several city districts and specific plans were considered.

These efforts were supported by Team Machizukuri, an association organized by members of the national government's "Reconstruction Design Council in Response to the Great East Japan Earthquake" Study Group (headed by Representative Director Professor Takashi Onishi of the Graduate School of the University of Tokyo). Team Machizukuri utilizes the knowledge and experience of experts from diverse fields, including urban planning, and provides a range of advice to the Ishinomaki Town Development Study Committee, acting as a platform linking industry, academia, and government as well as central and local governments in order to achieve the reconstruction of towns in the disaster zone.

Through such an exchange of ideas and information within the local community, the Compact City Ishinomaki—Central Town Reconstruction Council (Advisers: Ishinomaki City Mayor Hiroshi Kameyama, Ishinomaki City Council Chairman Masaaki Abe, and Professor Takashi Onishi of the Graduate School of the University of Tokyo; President: Ishinomaki Chamber of Commerce and Industry Chairman Toru Asano; Vice-President: urban planner Mariko Saigo) was organized in December 2011 in order to coordinate the various independent review committees and comprehensively consider and promote regional reconstruction development for the central town district as a whole (Fig. 4.2).

2.4.2 Ishinomaki Regional Reconstruction Development Aimed at "COOL"

According to its by-laws, the purpose of the Compact City Ishinomaki Central Town Reconstruction Council is as follows.

> The purpose of this council is to comprehensively consider the reconstruction and improvement of the central town of Ishinomaki City in cooperation with land owners, leaseholders, and other related persons and groups with the aim of creating a leading-edge model for sustainable regional development in response to the decreasing population, declining birth rate, and aging of society—issues that it is feared will grow even more serious in the future—as well as promoting regional development appropriate for Ishinomaki's landscape, history, and culture and contributing to local development.

Since before the earthquake, many areas of the disaster zone were facing numerous problems, such as stagnation of the local economy, declining employment, decreasing cohesion in local communities, and weakening local culture, and Ishinomaki was no exception. Here regional reconstruction development will not succeed with just improvements made to structures made of concrete: this is the basic concept of Ishinomaki regional reconstruction development.

Specifically, the most important points in local rehabilitation are utilizing Ishinomaki's local resources and unique features/characteristics to the maximum,

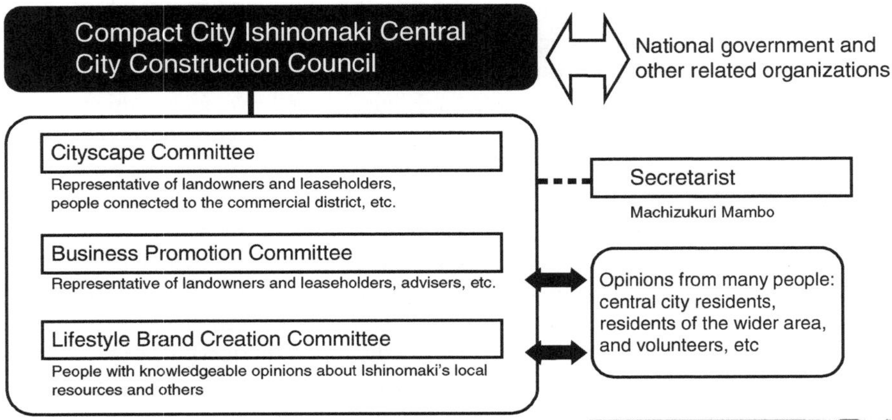

- Name: Compact City Ishinomaki Central City Construction Council
- Date of Establishment: December 20, 2011
- Officers
  - Advisers
    - Hiroshi Kameyama (Mayor of Ishinomaki City)
    - Masaaki Abe (Chairman of the Ishinomaki City Council)
    - Takashi Onishi (University of Tokyo Professor)
  - President
    - Toru Asano (Chairman of the Ishinomaki Chamber of Commerce and Industry)
  - Vice-Presidents
    - Yasuaki Onoda (Tohoku University Professor), Mariko Saigo (Representative, Machizukuri Company Sheep Network), Munenori Goto (President, Ishinomaki Tourist Association), and Masatoshi Saijo (President, Machizukuri Mambo)
- Purposes
  - Enhancing reconstruction in cooperation with land owners, leaseholders, and other related persons
  - Creating a leading-edge model for sustainable urban development
  - Promoting urban and cityscape development appropriate for Ishinomaki's scenery, history, and culture
  - Enhancing reconstruction in cooperation with land owners, leaseholders, and other related persons and groups
- Cityscape Committee
  - Considers the overall state of the city from the main perspective of landscape design
- Business Promotion Committee
  - Promotes redevelopment, etc., that is useful in creating more comfortable central city living environments using advantageous business methods
- Lifestyle Brand Creation Committee
  - Building an Ishinomaki lifestyle brand by polishing "Ishinomaki-ness" and diffusing information

Fig. 4.2 Implementation system for regional reconstruction development projects (Ishinomaki side)

mobilizing the collective effort of the community, and reconstructing self-sustaining and sustainable regional development frameworks; and it is imperative that new commercial and business enterprises are created in the buildings created through reconstruction.

From this perspective, the Compact City Ishinomaki—Central Town Reconstruction Council aimed to look again at the Ishinomaki lifestyle and the "Ishinomakiness" within local products and by refining these unique characteristics communicate them around the country and around the world as something "COOL." Currently, local producers, designers, and creators are also participating

Fig. 4.3 Aiming for "cool" regional development: fervent discussions continuing late into the night

in and promoting the council, which is endeavouring to develop shops and facilities aimed at industrialising the so-called Ishinomaki lifestyle itself (Team Machizukuri 2012).

2.4.3 Concrete Image of Regional Development

As described above, in Tokyo, Team Machizukuri took an educated approach to regional reconstruction development; in Ishinomaki City, through teamwork that can truly be called *kizuna* (bonding)—by which actual projects were carried out through a coordinated government/private sector system while respecting as far as possible the wishes of residents—fervent discussions carrying late into the night are being held regularly and central town redevelopment plans are proceeding (Fig. 4.3).

Of these, plans are taking shape for six central areas near the Kyu-kitakami River covering an area of approximately 4.5 ha, and for four of these areas housing improvements are planned to enable these to be used as disaster public housing. In Ishinomaki City there are a total of 13,500 temporary shelters (7,000 temporary homes and 6,500 rented temporary homes), and the Ishinomaki City Office has drawn up plans to build 4,000 homes as disaster public housing; the residents of the remaining 9,500 temporary homes are faced with the difficult choice of either purchasing homes themselves or renting. Accordingly, this central town redevelopment can be said to be a model for realising a "compact city" that combines housing and industry.

Fig. 4.4 Images of the cityscape of a safe and secure compact city that attracts industry

As an example, the plan for Tachimachi 1-chome envisions constructing buildings with parking areas and shops on the first floor, shops and offices on the second floor as artificial ground, and housing on the third floor and above in order to avoid the danger of tsunamis in an area that includes the Ishinomaki Chamber of Commerce and Industry. Overall, buildings are to be low-rise structures comprising three to four floors, with sections facing the road comprising mainly shops and offices and inner sections comprising housing (Fig. 4.4).

Again, sustainable regional development that responds to the decreasing population, declining birth rate, and ageing of society is an issue common to regional areas throughout Japan, not only Ishinomaki, and regional development and cityscape development appropriate for the landscape, history, and culture of each region need to be promoted, and thus industries that fully utilise Ishinomaki's local resources as well as the area's unique features and characteristics must be expanded.

Central towns in regional areas need to proactively fulfil the function of becoming intermediaries between producers and consumers by transforming beautiful cityscapes, with delicious cuisine, and a lifestyle emphasising stylish household goods and fashion into a unique local brand—for example, community restaurants and cafes/food stores handling local foodstuffs; craftwork and furniture created by local artisans; and galleries displaying and selling historical and cultural resources.

The disaster zone has the potential to become a leading-edge model for such regional development, and now is the time that industry, government, and academia as well as central, local government need to work together as one with teamwork reflecting strong *kizuna* (bonds) to take on this challenge. It is possible to transform the plight caused by the earthquake into an opportunity.

2.4.4 Future Schedule

Recently, the Ishinomaki City Office has received approval as a Special Central City Rehabilitation Zone for the redevelopment of the central city district with the aim of attracting commerce and tourism as well as healthcare and welfare services. Thus, this project also matches the city's thinking, and from this perspective the City Office is currently showing a positive attitude towards promoting the project.

Looking ahead, a city plan will be decided as early as autumn 2012, and the project is proceeding with the aim of commencing construction in March 2013.

Two years after the earthquake disaster, regional reconstruction development—which for disaster zone residents means enabling them to return home with peace of mind, restoring their community, and providing places for them to work—is finally and actually starting. This is truly a "light of hope," and there are high hopes for the realisation of projects done with speed.

2.5 *Utilisation of HIT in Regional Reconstruction Development*

From this perspective, it can be said that HIT schemes can be useful financial tools in the implementation of such regional reconstruction development.

2.5.1 "Goodwill" Financing

First of all, there is the matter of "goodwill" financing. The Ishinomaki Regional Reconstruction Development Project aims to achieve industrialization by communicating to the rest of the country and the world the "Cool Ishinomakiness" of Ishinomaki living and local products—that is, the city's lifestyle itself—including creating beautiful scenery through the establishment of design codes.

In order to attract actual commerce and improve the cityscape, financing sympathetic to these "intentions" is indispensable, and so there is a need for new financing channels that have risk tolerance characteristics that differ from those of existing financial institutions. In other words, expectations are high for the use of HIT by "fans" that will sustain these reconstruction efforts—that is, funding that focuses more on supporting the reconstruction efforts themselves than on returns.

2.5.2 Direct Participation by Individual Investors via the Internet

In addition, there is a lack of marketing and poor dissemination of information about many products of not only Ishinomaki but also other regions of the disaster zone, despite their appeal as local resources backed by history and culture. Conversely, it is also believed there is tremendous room for uncovering latent demand, and HIT schemes that advertise the appeal of local products directly to individuals via the Internet could be very effective tools for expanding the "fan base" for local products.

2.5.3 Financing with a Sense of Speed

Furthermore, regional reconstruction development demands speed. In order to restore a city's vibrancy, it is essential that the return of appealing stores and retail businesses as well as new locations is promoted swiftly.

That said, procuring funds for this is problematic with the existing finance, and so new procurement methods are now required. Even if it is a small sum or on a small scale, regional reconstruction development is required quickly, and the use of HIT is thought to be extremely effective, as the example of Music Securities, Inc.'s Securité Disaster Area Support Fund shows.

2.5.4 Mezzanine Financing

The nature of the funds is also important. In regional reconstruction development, even if tenants for stores and retail businesses are assembled swiftly, they need to be prepared for the possibility that it may take a substantial amount of time for the city to regain its vitality.

In November 2011, the Securité Disaster Area Support Fund[2] was deemed by the Financial Services Agency to "be able to accredit loans deemed to have sufficient capital capacity (equity loans)," receiving so-called "mezzanine approval."

For eligible business operators in the disaster zone, this approval meant that the financing they received from the Securité Disaster Area Support Fund (a silent partner deposit) was capital under certain conditions, contributing to the balance sheet improvement of eligible businesses facing a lack of capital.

Furthermore, the fund is expected to make it easier for businesses to receive financing from banks and other financial institutions, and so there are even greater expectations that this will boost regional reconstruction development. From such a perspective, HIT schemes are sure to become powerful financial tools for reconstruction.

---

[2] See footnote 1 of Chap. 3.

3 The Kokusyu (Sake and Shochu) Project

Next, I will introduce a case that shows the utilization of HIT, in view of its characteristics, as a policy already adopted by the government.

Sake and *shochu* (including Okinawan Awamori) are a Japanese *kokusyu* (national drink) and are created with not only native products such as rice and water but they are also, in a manner of speaking, the "crystallisation of Japaneseness" epitomised by the Japanese climate and Japanese attention to detail and sensitivity. However, their domestic consumption has been decreasing, and the number of sake breweries in Japan continues to dwindle. That is to say, HIT schemes are a financial tool that can be utilised to overcome this *kokusyu* crisis.

3.1 Local Economics Aimed at Global Marketing

3.1.1 Moves by the National Government and Local Government Authorities

Domestic demand for *kokusyu* is on a downward trend, and this situation is expected to become even more serious as the Japanese population decreases in the future. However, looking overseas opens up tremendous market potential with the world population increasing, developing countries achieving economic growth, and a worldwide Japanese cuisine boom. Cognizant of these issues, the national government has expressed the need to "open up markets through global marketing with an eye to not only domestic but also overseas demand" by improving the export environment for *kokusyu* and other alcoholic beverages produced in Japan as one of its Strategies to Revitalise Japan (approved by the Cabinet in July 2012) (Table 4.3).

Local government authorities—for example, Kumamoto Prefecture—have also been scouting for veteran businesspeople with abundant overseas experience and networks of personal contacts and strengthening their systems for selling prefecture products, including *kokusyu*) overseas. Saga Prefecture has established a Metropolitan Marketing Headquarters in its Tokyo office and is also proactively endeavouring to attract overseas tourists.

3.1.2 Need for "Locally Generated Global Marketing"

In local economies faced with a dwindling numbers and requiring demand from abroad there is a need for the potential value of local products to be recognized and expanded on the world market—that is to say, there is need for "locally generated global marketing." To achieve this, regions need to display tremendous entrepreneurial spirit while making the most of their various traditions and strengths, actively take on challenges with innovation and ingenuity, and respond flexibly.

Table 4.3 Efforts towards locally generated global marketing. "Strategies to Revitalize Japan" (approved by the Cabinet on July 30, 2012)

(Priority measures: promotion of agricultural, forestry, and fisheries product exports and expansion of overseas markets for Japanese "foodstuffs", such as Kokusyu)
In order to raise the export amount for agricultural, forestry, and fisheries products and foodstuffs—which has dropped due to the effects of the nuclear power plant accident—to a level of one trillion yen by 2020, Japan will strengthen efforts to promote agricultural, forestry, and fisheries products and foodstuffs using such methods as lobbying other countries to relax import regulations, construction of marketing system as a national strategy, acceleration of quarantine discussions, and the diffusion of Japanese food culture overseas
Furthermore, efforts will be made **as a model measure for opening up markets through global marketing with an eye to not only domestic but also international demand to comprehensively improve the environment for promoting exports of Kokusyu and other Japanese alcoholic beverages** through public–private sector collaboration, including such measures as eliminating or relaxing import regulations, lowering customs duties, and strengthening sales to other countries by utilizing diplomatic missions abroad and organizations such as JETRO
Through the accumulation and utilization of successful examples of efforts such as those described above, overseas markets for Japanese "foodstuffs" will expand

3.2 The Kokusyu Project as a Model Case

3.2.1 The Kokusyu Project as a Local Revitalization Strategy

The overseas expansion of *kokusyu* and other Japanese alcoholic beverages, which have become fused with Japanese food culture, is expected to have a synergistic effect, expanding overseas demand for not only Japanese foodstuffs but also traditional crafts such as sake cups and tableware. It will also prompt the expansion of production of rice and other ingredients, not only contributing to the revitalization of agriculture but also leading to the preservation of regional environments through the protection of water, which is another vital ingredient of alcohol.

Furthermore, sake breweries are located in prefectures throughout the country and from days of old have been closely associated with the business activities of local people, in many cases playing a central role in local society. If *kokusyu* can be recognized internationally as one of the attractions of Japan and overseas exports of *kokusyu* expanded, local revitalisation centred on sake breweries can be expected.

Also, in many cases sake breweries are located in traditional Japanese buildings *saka-gura*. Together with the surrounding townscape, sake breweries complete the traditional Japanese lanscape. Blending sake culture with local food culture and fusing it with traditional crafts and local tourism has the potential to attract lovers and handlers of *kokusyu* both in Japan and overseas and to act as a spark for local revitalisation. Developing "sake brewery tourism" can be expected to increase the number of sake lovers with a storyline directly tied to Japanese culture, leading also to an increase in the brand value of *kokusyu* and exports (Fig. 4.5).

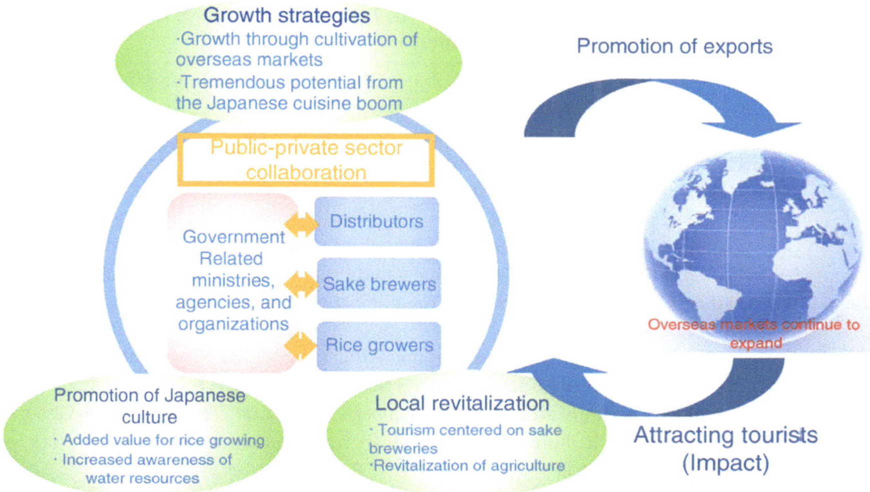

Fig. 4.5 The "Kokusyu Project" as a regional development strategy

3.2.2 Government Organizational System

Consequently, the government has come together to begin promoting the Kokusyu Project as a model case for "locally generated global marketing."

The Cabinet Secretariat's National Strategy Office launched the Enjoy Japanese Kokusyu Project on May 11, 2012 with the aim of promoting the Kokusyu Project and established a panel of advisers (council) as the advisory body for the State Minister in Charge of National Strategy. Following discussions held over several meetings, a committee for the Program for the Promotion of Kokusyu Experts was formed on September 4, 2012 (Table 4.4).

Furthermore, based on the committee's discussions, the First Export Promotion of Kokusyu Conference was held on September 18, 2012 and a promotional system was launched under the State Minister in Charge of National Strategy comprising the Parliamentary Secretary of Cabinet Office and cabinet councillors as well as the heads of various bureaus and councillor-level officials. With government promotional organizations such as Japan External Trade Organization (JETRO) and Japan National Tourist Organization (JNTO) also participating in the committee, expectations are high for the establishment of a workable system.

Table 4.4 Promotional system for the "Program for the Promotion of Kokusyu Exports". National government "Export Promotion of Kokusyu Conference"

Chairman	Parliamentary Secretary of the Cabinet Office advising the State Minister in Charge of National Strategy
Members	Cabinet Secretariat Cabinet Councilor
	Cabinet Secretariat Cabinet Public Relations Secretary
	Cabinet Secretariat Intellectual Property Strategy Promotion Bureau Director-General
	Cabinet Office Minister's Secretariat Senior Deputy Secretary General
	Cabinet Office Okinawa Development and Promotion Bureau Director-General
	Ministry of Internal Affairs and Communications Councilor for Generating Regional Strength
	Ministry for Foreign Affairs Economic Affairs Bureau Director-General
	National Tax Agency Commissioner's Secretariat Deputy Director-General
	Agency for Cultural Affairs Commissioner's Secretariat Deputy Director-General
	Ministry of Agriculture, Forestry and Fisheries Food Industry Bureau Director-General
	Ministry of Economy, Trade and Industry Commerce and Information Policy Bureau Director-General
	Japan Tourism Agency Deputy Director General

3.3 Utilization of HIT for the Kokusyu Project

3.3.1 Orientations of the Government Council

The above-mentioned Program for the Promotion of Kokusyu Exports indicates its orientation regarding such issues as "construction of marketing strategies," "establishment of *kokusyu* brands," "improvement of export environments," and "expansion of overseas sales channels," and with regard to fund procurement, "use of HIT has been indicated as a means of 'strengthening the foundation of industries supporting the export of kokusyu.'"

When sake brewers expand their business activities, a smooth supply of operating capital and capital investment funds is necessary, but the burden on small and medium-sized brewers is large. For this reason, in addition to government financial institution system financing and trade insurance and other allowances for *kokusyu* brewers and distributors, utilisation of HIT would surely be valuable as a concrete fund procurement support measure (Conference for the Promotion of Kokusyu Exports 2012: http://www.npu.go.jp/policy/policy04/archive12_001.html#haifu) (Table 4.5).

3.3.2 Potential for Utilization of HIT

Music Securities, Inc. has already set up several "sake brewery funds" and is achieving substantial results. However, brewers clarifying their business plans and management policies and bringing in individual small investors as "investment with a face" can be another useful fund procurement method. Long-term borrowing from

Table 4.5 Program for the Promotion of Kokusyu Exports: use of Hometown Investment Trust funds (approved by the Conference to Promote the Enjoy Japanese Kokusyu Project on September 4, 2012) (support for fund procurement for exports)

When a sake brewer expands their business activities, a smooth supply of operating capital and capital investment funds is necessary, but the burden on small and medium brewers is large
For this reason, Kokusyu brewers and distributors utilize government financial institution system financing and trade insurance to promote exports. Moreover, utilization of organizations supporting the transformation of agriculture and fisheries into growth industries for supporting the export of Kokusyu and other Japanese alcoholic beverages as well as the utilization of Organization for Small and Medium-sized Enterprises and Regional Innovation investment funds (limited partnerships for investment) should also be considered in the future
In recent years, private sector funds for Japanese breweries have been set up, and brewers clarifying their business plans and management policies and bringing in private-sector investors is another useful fund procurement method. In such cases, utilization of the "Hometown Investment (local revitalization small-sum investment) Platform"—a measure to support small fund activities that contribute to local revitalization whose construction the Cabinet Secretariat is currently promoting—may also be considered

banks is difficult in the case of breweries producing *junmaisyu* sake (a superior type of sake using no distilled alcohol), which takes several years to mature, since it is not possible to collect income during the maturation period and equity loans are necessary. However, HIT can make this possible.

More than anything else, increasing a product's fan base is tremendously effective. Disseminating information via the Internet is an effective tool not only for procuring funds but also advertising the appeal of *kokusyu*, and also contributes greatly to the expansion of the *kokusyu* market, which is now facing a crisis.

In promoting the Kokusyu Project in future, it would be desirable to expand the market scale for HIT and set up funds aimed at sake-related businesses in each region. As we meet the arrival of depopulation and internal demand peaks, the key to local revitalisation will be how effectively products can be expanded into overseas markets. Expectations are high for the fields in which HIT is used as a finance scheme to encourage efforts towards locally generated global marketing to expand further, as well as for the public and private sectors to unite in their efforts in this endeavour.

References

Development Bank of Japan (2012) Report of the regional reconstruction development working group, March 2012

Hasue T (2012) Reconstruction support utilizing the special recovery area act from a finance perspective. Financial Affairs (February)

Komatsu M (2012) Towards the construction of Hometown Investment Platforms. Hometown Investment Platform Promotional conference, 2 August 2012

Murate S (2012) Current status of and efforts at reconstruction after the Great East Japan Earthquake. Chiho Zaimu (August)

Team Machizukuri (2012) Regional reconstruction development through a three-point approach: sustainable urban development in a depopulating society, June 2012

Chapter 5
HIT as a Form of Microfinance in Asia

Yuka Morita

In Chaps. 3 and 4, we discussed the achievements and potential of Hometown Investment Trust (HIT) Funds in Japan. This chapter takes a look at the application of HIT-type funds as a form of microfinance in other parts of Asia.

1 Microfinance

1.1 The Microfinance Market

Microfinance is the collective name for financial services provided on a small scale. These services include not just loans, but also insurance, savings, and remittances. The services are mainly directed to the poorer segment of the population in developing countries. The institutions that engage in these services locally are referred to as microfinance institutions (MFI). The Microfinance Investment Funds for Millennium Development Goals that are managed by Music Securities, Inc., is a fund for the purpose of financing this kind of MFIs.

According to a report from the Microfinance Summit Campaign (Reed 2011), there were more than 3,500 approved MFIs in the world reaching approximately 190 million clients. When institutions that have not received approval are included, the total number of MFIs is said by some to be around 10,000. The balance of microfinance loans made was 70 billion dollars or more as of 2009 (Fig. 5.1).

Y. Morita (✉)
Music Securities Inc., Tokyo, Japan
e-mail: morita@musicsecurities.com

N. Yoshino and S. Kaji (eds.), *Hometown Investment Trust Funds: A Stable Way to Supply Risk Capital*, DOI 10.1007/978-4-431-54309-1_5, © Springer Japan 2013

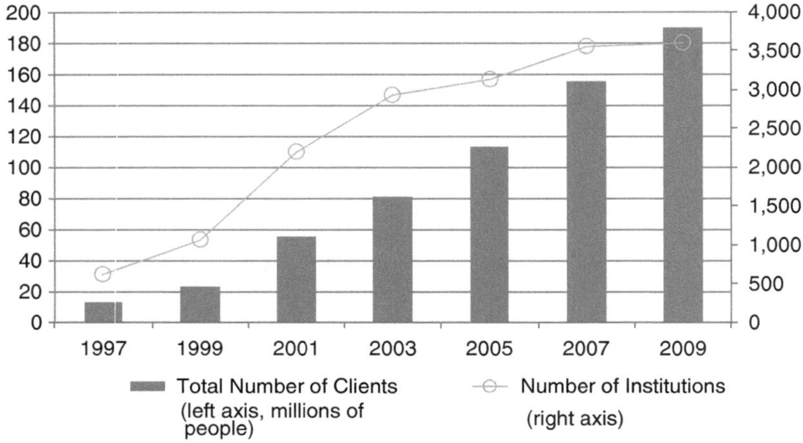

Fig. 5.1 Number of MFIs and number of clients. *Source*: The microfinance summit campaign

1.2 Microfinance Investment

In general, microfinance investment refers to investments made in MFIs. When an independent investment entity includes multiple investors and 50% or more of its non-cash assets are invested in MFIs, it is termed a microfinance investment vehicle (MIV). Of the types of MIV investment, including both direct and indirect together, 85% or more consist of investments in debt instruments, and 14.5% are investments in equity instruments. The Microfinance Investment Funds for Millennium Development Goals belong under debt investments. It consists of funds raised from small individual investors, and it is characterized by a distribution ratio, corresponding to interest, that is determined every fiscal year according to the performance of the investment project (Fig. 5.2).

The MIV market is showing continuing growth, but it has slowed down since the financial crisis. The MIV asset growth rate is anticipated to be about 19% in 2012. Looking by region, 41% of the MIV investment amount goes to Eastern Europe and Central Asia, but the growth rate is highest in investments going to Sub-Saharan Africa, which grew 54% in 2010 and 41% in 2011 (Fig. 5.3).

Looking at the state of the microfinance investment market, we see a bias in investment funds, many of which are concentrated in major investments. According to the Grameen Foundation, 90% of the money flowing into the microfinance sector is said to go to the 150 largest MFIs whilst 10% goes to 9,850 small to medium-sized MFIs (Grameen Foundation 2010). In terms of amounts, the average size of an MIV investment is 1.8 million dollars, its average period is 2 years, and some 30% is denominated in loc.l currencies. This investment size is too large for medium to small MFIs.

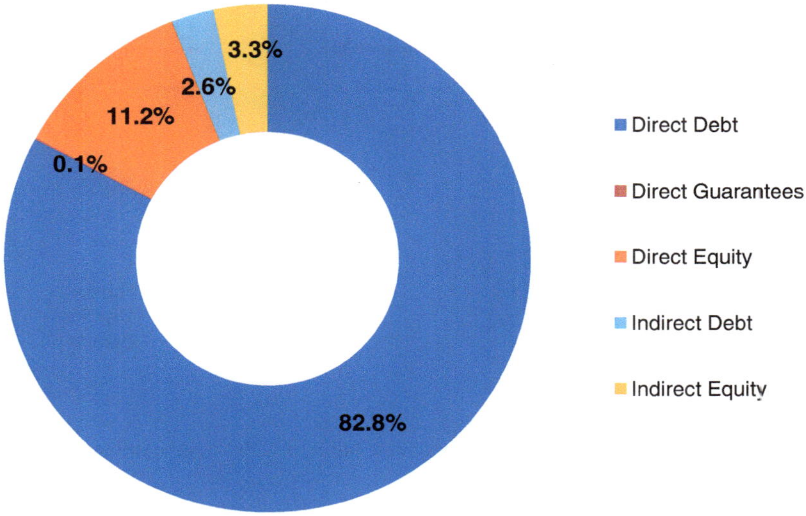

Fig. 5.2 Financial instruments, % of microfinance portfolio. *Source*: Symbiotics Research & Advisory (2012)

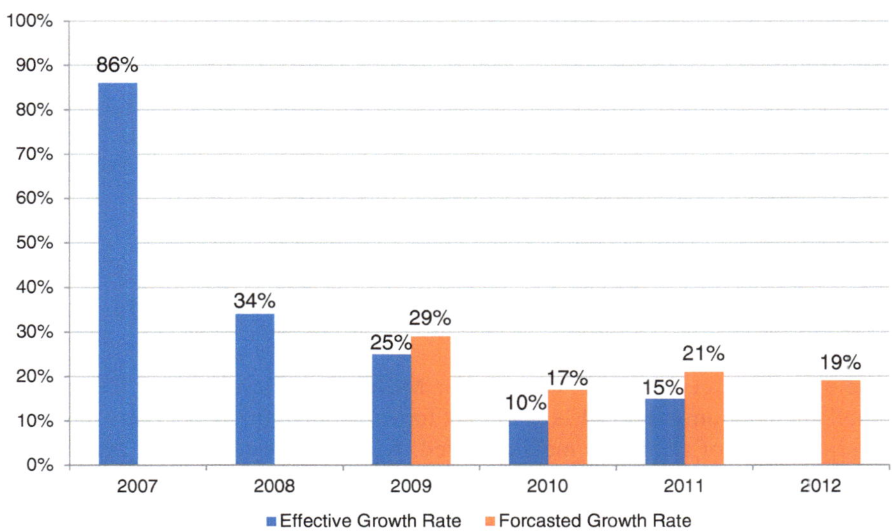

Fig. 5.3 MIV total asset growth. *Source*: Symbiotics Research & Advisory (2012)

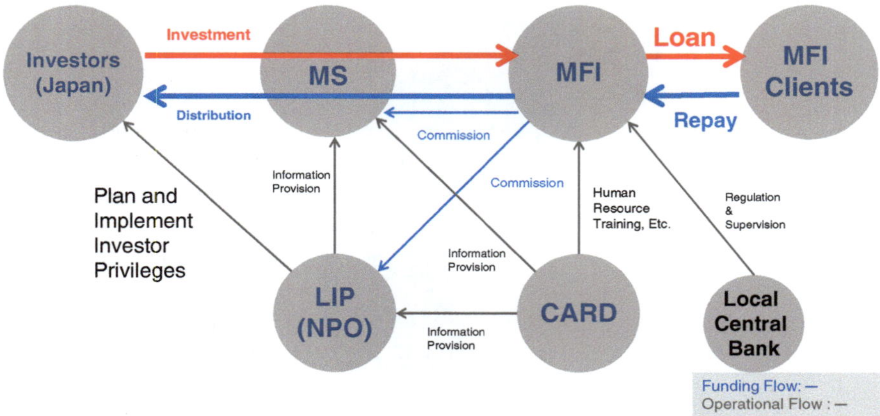

Fig. 5.4 Mechanism of the microfinance investment funds for millennium development goals

2 Microfinance Investment Funds for Millennium Development Goals

Figure 5.4 shows the mechanism of the Microfinance Investment Funds for Millennium Development Goals. Money is raised in small amounts from individuals in Japan, who invest in units of 30,000 yen. The money is passed through Music Securities to the local MFI that operates that fund. Loans and other regular operations are then implemented by the MFI, and the funds are repaid after 3 years. Dividends are paid out annually according to the performance of MFI management.

The mechanism of the Microfinance Investment Funds for Millennium Development Goals has the three following characteristics:

2.1 Direct Investments in Small and Medium-Sized MFIs

The Microfinance Investment Funds for Millennium Development Goals take small and medium-sized MFIs as targets for investment in order to also meet the funding needs of small and medium-sized. As to what size range is involved, a Cambodian MFI called SAMIC, which is one of the recipients of investment from the Microfinance Investment Funds for Millennium Development Goals, offers an example. In terms of the amount of outstanding loans to clients, SAMIC ranks eleventh of the 33 registered MFIs in Cambodia (as of the end of June 2012; in Cambodia there are 60 or more additional MFIs that have not been registered). As shown in Fig. 5.7, SAMIC has over 12,000 clients and approximately 150 employees.

Another MFI of the same scale as SAMIC is Seilanithih. The MFI known as TYM in Vietnam was founded in 1992 by the Vietnam Women's Union, the official

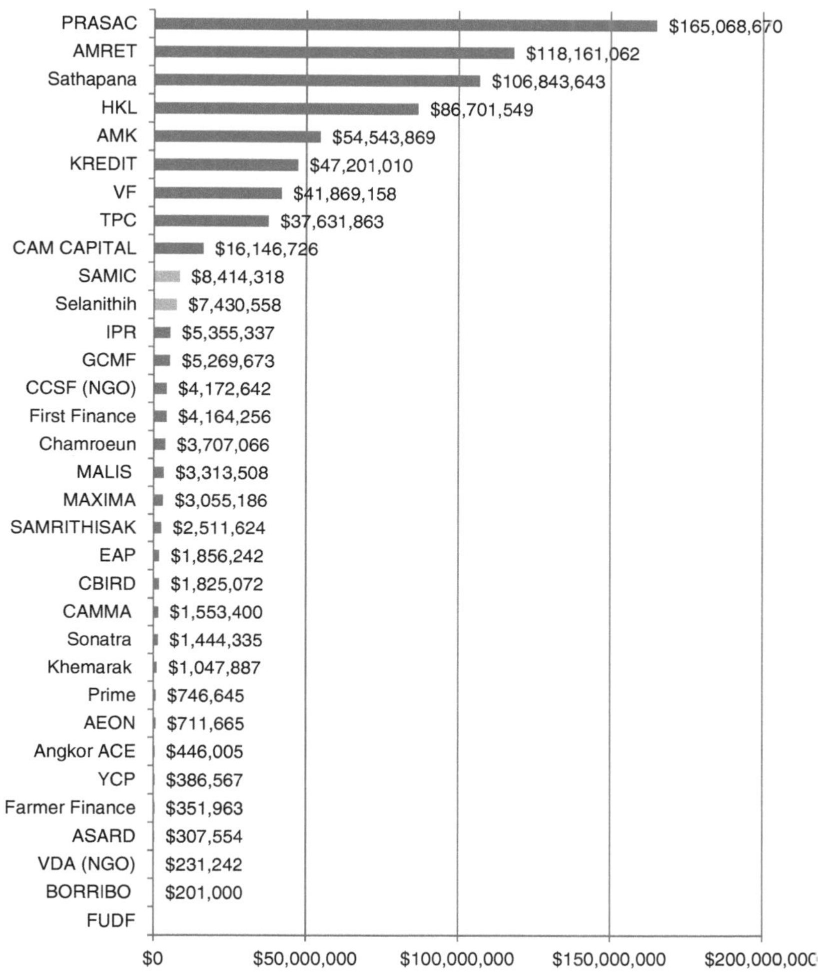

Fig. 5.5 Outstanding loans by MFIs in Cambodia (as of end June 2012; excludes largest institution ACLEDA)

Vietnamese organization for women, in order to support the government plan to eradicate poverty. It ranks fourth in terms of total loans (as of the end of 2011), but when fund planning was underway (end of October 2010), it was the only MFI in Vietnam that had acquired a microfinance license. A conspicuously large MFI is the Vietnam Bank for Social Policies (VBSP), which is a governmental financial institution.

Thus, although the MFIs selected as targets for investment are small to medium in size, they are institutions that have a record of performance, that have been registered by the national government, and that are obligated to undergo external audits (Figs. 5.5 and 5.6) (Table 5.1).

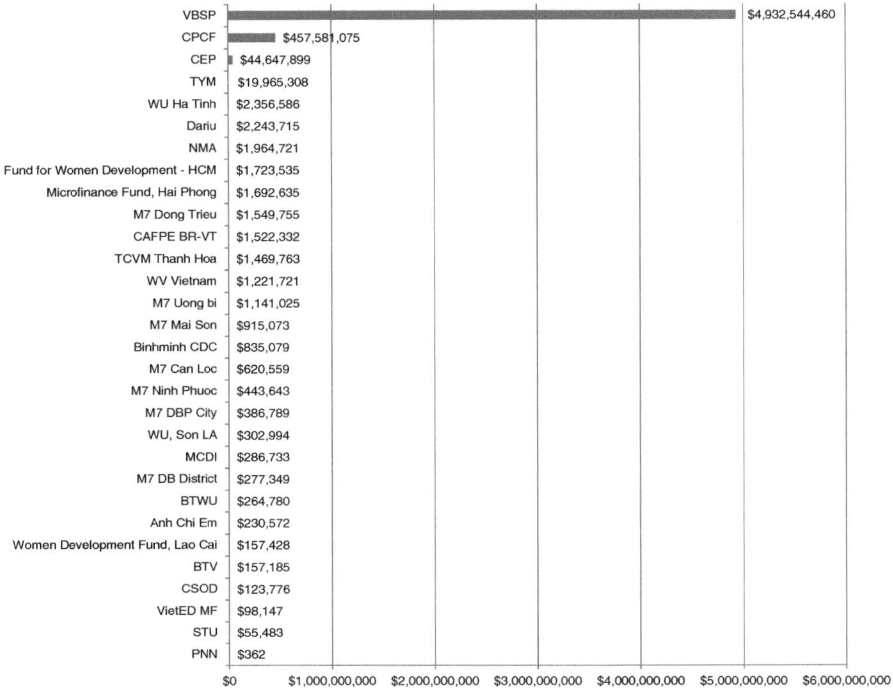

Fig. 5.6 Outstanding loans by MFIs in Vietnam (as of end 2011). *Source*: Mix market

Table 5.1 Overview of MFI recipients of investments from microfinance investment funds for millennium development goals

MFI	Samic	Seilanithih	TYM
Country	Cambodia	Cambodia	Vietnam
Number of clients	12,492	12,431	73,246
Percentage of women clients	80%	70%	100%
Loans outstanding	$8,414,318	$7,430,558	$19,965,308
Percentage with payments delayed 30 days or more	0.93%	1.40%	0.02%
Average loan size	$674	$598	$275
Number of employees	146	203	339
Registration status	Registered (33 MFIs are registered in Cambodia. There are also 60 or more MFIs that are unregistered or NGOs)	Registered	Registered (First acquired license as micro finance institution in Vietnam in October 2010)

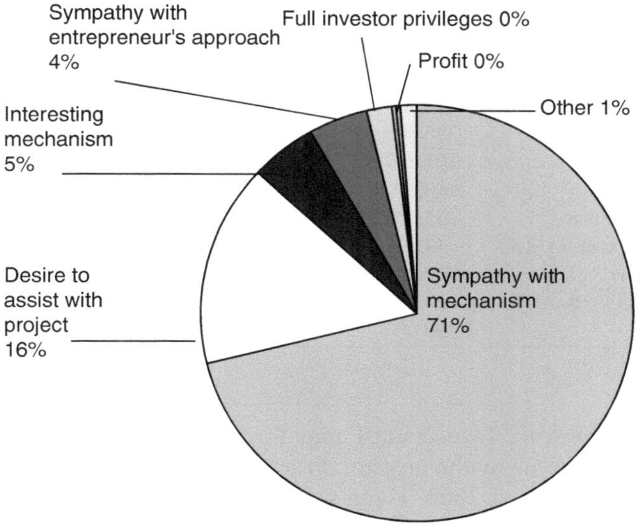

Fig. 5.7 Reasons for buying in to the microfinance investment funds for millennium development goals

2.2 *Small Investments from Private Individuals*

The second characteristic of the Microfinance Investment Funds for Millennium Development Goals is that this fund takes small investments from private individuals. Money is raised in small amounts from individuals in Japan, who invest in units of 30,000 yen, and that money is sent to the on-site MFI. The investment motivation was 90% stated in such terms as, "because I felt sympathetic to the idea of an arrangement that lets us help not with donations but with investments" and "because I want to provide support [to MFIs] across national boundaries." Virtually nobody invested out of the desire for a financial return.

The Microfinance Investment Funds for Millennium Development Goals therefore take steps to make itself more "an investment with a visible face" by giving investors monthly reports on the financial status of the MFI invested in that also introduced MFI staff members and clients with photographs. They also organised study tours to actual sites and set up opportunities for investors to have contact with staff members and clients of the MFI recipients of their investments. In December 2012, they will hold Micro Business Awards in which business borrowers with the most meritorious achievement are chosen by vote and given commendations. The winners will be invited to Japan on a business trip that includes occasions for exchange with investors. Programs were also previously carried on to invite staff members of investment recipient MFIs to Japan so that investors could hear directly what the people involved had to say (Fig. 5.7).

Table 5.2 SAMIC shareholders

Shareholder names	Amount (USD)	Number of shares held (shares)	% of ownership (%)
CMI-International Holding	500,000	50,000	38.46
CHC-NGO	330,000	33,000	25.38
Dr. Sok Thim	201,000	20,100	15.46
CARD-NGO	100,000	10,000	7.69
Mr. King Kap Kalyan	65,000	6,500	5.00
Staff Association of SAMIC	44,000	4,400	3.38
Dr. Chiv Bunthy	40,000	4,000	3.08
Dr. Jaime Aristotle B. Alip	20,000	2,000	1.54
Total	1,300,000	130,000	100.00

In the Microfinance Investment Funds for Millennium Development Goals, exchange risk is borne by the investor. Past exchange rate movements show that as of the end of August 2009, 1 yen was worth 43.69 riel, so 30,000 yen was 1,310,700 riel. As of the end of August 2012, the rise in the yen has made 1 yen worth 51.71 riel, so that the same 1,310,700 riel is now worth 25,347 yen. This exchange risk that must fall on someone falls on the investor. No doubt this is only possible because these are small investments by multiple private individuals who are not motivated by desire for financial return so much as by understanding of or sympathy with the mechanism and desire to aid the MFI or business in a developing country.

2.3 *Collaboration with Partners*

The third characteristic of the Microfinance Investment Funds for Millennium Development Goals is that it involves collaboration with partners. Investment in small to medium-sized MFIs typically entails relative credit risk and difficulty in searching for prospective projects. The Microfinance Investment Funds for Millennium Development Goals, however, seek to resolve these problems by collaborating with CARD, the largest MFI in the Philippines. SAMIC, Seilanithih, and TYM, which are recipients of investment from the Microfinance Investment Funds for Millennium Development Goals to date, have all either received human resource training or start-up support from CARD, or are affiliated with CARD. All these investments were introduced through CARD. Table 5.2 shows the SAMIC shareholders, and we see that CARD holds 7.69% of the shares in SAMIC.

The existence of this fund is also based on its collaboration with the authorized non-profit organization known as Living in Peace (LIP). Specifically, LIP engages in MFI studies, fund planning, creation of analyst reports, monitoring, activities to spread the recognition of microfinance, and so on. Music Securities, Inc., which is a Type II Financial Instruments Business Operator, makes decisions on fund plans and engages in origination, sales, solicitation, management, investor relations, and other such activities. In microfinance investment, one factor involved in the concentration of investment funds in the major MFIs is the necessity to increase the amounts invested and recover investment costs. If investment costs are not reduced, it will become more difficult to invest in small and medium-sized MFIs. Collaboration with this kind of non-profit organization (NPO) is therefore essential.

3 The Track Record of Microfinance Investment Funds

Between the founding of Japan's first microfinance fund in 2009 and the time of this writing in September 2012, five funds have been originated here. Cambodia 1 sent funds to the Siem Reap branch of the SAMIC MFI in Cambodia, Cambodia 2 to the Kep branch of that same MFI, and Cambodia 3 to the Chamkar Leu branch of the Seilanithih MFI in Cambodia. As of September 2012, the Vietnam 1 fund, which will invest in the TYM MFI in Vietnam, and Cambodia 4, which will invest in SAMIC in Cambodia, were canvassing for investors. These funds have found a total of 1,000 or more participants, and the money they have raised amounts to a total of approximately 100 million yen (Fig. 5.8).

The dividends from the various funds are calculated by different methods. What they have in common is that the dividend rate is determined each fiscal year by the performance of the project receiving investment in terms of a reference year. The dividend rates also have upper limits set.

In the case of the first fund, Cambodia 1, the dividend rate is calculated as follows.

<Dividend Rate>

The calculation of the Dividend Rate is described below in a formulaic format:

1. If the net profit of the fiscal year is equal to or below net profit of the fiscal year 2008:

$$\text{Dividend Rate} = \left[\frac{\text{net profit of the fiscal year (ii)}}{\text{net profit of the fiscal year 2008(i)}}\right] \times 0.025 + 2.5\%$$

2. If net profit of the fiscal year exceeds net profit of the fiscal year 2008:

$$\text{Dividend Rate} = \left[\frac{\text{net profit of the fiscal year(ii)}}{\text{net profit of the fiscal year 2008(i)}}\right] \times 0.00026 + 5\%$$

Note: The project is the microfinance project implemented by SAMIC primarily through the Siem Reap Branch.

The net profits (i) and (ii) in the above formulas are as follows:

(i) Net profit of the Siem Reap Branch and any other relevant branches for fiscal year 2008

The net profits of the Siem Reap branch and any other relevant branches for fiscal year 2008, which provide the reference amount, are, when the branches

MFI	Cambodia ONE	Cambodia 2	Cambodia 3	Vietnam ONE	Cambodia 4
	SAMIC Limited Siem Reap Branch	SAMIC Limited Kep Branch	Seilanithih Chamkar Leu Branch	TYM Whole Company	SAMIC Limited Whole Company
Subscription Period	**September 2009 –** November 2009	**December 2009 –** March 2010	**March 2011 –** August 2011	**From February 2012 (underway)**	**From June 2012** (underway)
Accounting Period	**January 2010-December 2012**	**April 2010-December 2012**	**From month after money sent to December 2013**	**From month after money sent to April 2015**	**From month after money sent to May 2016**
Distribution	**Lump sum**	**Lump sum**	**Annual**	**Annual**	**Annual**
Amount Raised	**24.6 million yen**	**14.64 million yen**	**31.11 million yen**	**22.23 million yen (as of end September)**	**5.85 million yen (as of end September)**
Number of Investors	**293 people**	**197 people**	**353 people**	**316 people (as of end September)**	**74 people (as of end September)**

Fig. 5.8 The track record of microfinance investment funds (as of end September 2012)

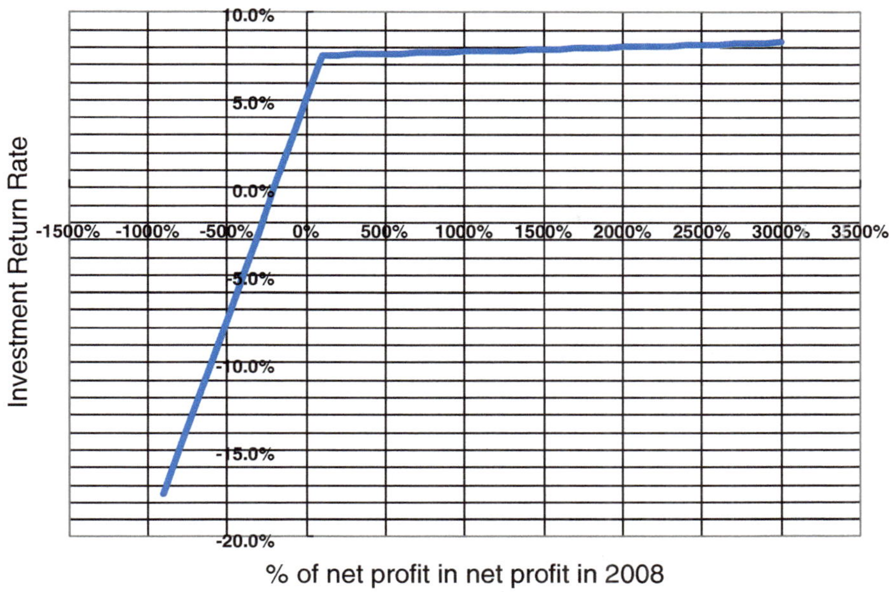

Fig. 5.9 Illustration of investment return

receiving funding from the project consist of the Siem Reap branch alone, the net profits of the Siem Reap branch. When the branches receiving funding include branches other than the Siem Reap branch, the net profits consist of the total net profits of the recipient branches. The formula for calculating the net profits of the Siem Reap branch and any other relevant branches for fiscal year 2008 is as follows.

Net profits of the Siem Reap Branch and any other relevant branches for fiscal year 2008:

(Net profit of the operator's company as a whole for fiscal year 2008) ×
[(Total loans from the Siem Reap branch, etc., in fiscal year 2008) /
(Total loans from the operator's company as a whole for fiscal year 2008)]

(ii) Net profit of the project for the fiscal year
The net profit of the project for the fiscal year is calculated from the audited report of financial results, which is submitted by the operator in May each year, or other such source using the following formula:

Net profit of the project for the fiscal year:

(Net profit of the operator's company as a whole for the fiscal year) ×
[(Total loans from the project for the fiscal year) /
(Total loans from the operator's company as a whole for the fiscal year)]

Details are recorded in the Tokumei Kumiai Agreement (Fig. 5.9).

Working from the above formulas, the performance to date in terms of interim dividend results comes out as follows:

Unit of investment, 30,000 yen
Fund investment amount per unit after deduction of fees, 325.08 USD
Amount of distribution paid per unit in fiscal year 2010, 13.51 USD
Amount of distribution paid per unit in fiscal year 2011, 16.42 USD

Note: Payment of the distribution amount is made in accordance with the Cambodia 1 Tokumei Kumiai Agreement, and it occurs one time at the end of the agreement period, not during the period.

Note: The amount of the investment made by this fund is repaid when the fund is redeemed. However, if the net profit for the project is a negative figure or under other such circumstances, the amount repaid may be less than the amount invested.

References

Grameen Foundation (2010) The making of a tiny loan, 7 May 2010, p. 23. http://grameenfoundation.org/sites/default/files/The-Making-of-a-Tiny-Loan.pdf. Accessed 31 Oct 2012

Reed LR (2011) State of the Microcredit Summit Campaign Report, p. 44. http://www.microcreditsummit.org/pubs/reports/socr/2011/SOCR_2011_EN_web.pdf. Accessed 31 Oct 2012

Symbiotics Research & Advisory (2012) 2012 Symbiotics MIV survey: Market Data & Peer Group Analysis, July 2012, pp. 7, 11. http://www.microfinancegateway.org/gm/document-1.9.59392/symbiotics-2012-miv-survey-report.pdf. Accessed 31 Oct 2012

Chapter 6
Concluding Remarks and the Way Forward

Shuhei Shiozawa

1 Introduction

This book is about Hometown Investment Trust (HIT) funds and other similar funds as a new form of financial intermediation. So far, we have discussed the funds' background, characteristics, achievements in Japan as well as some other Asian countries. We argued that HIT is more conducive to stability and more suitable for promoting recovery than the more traditional forms of financial intermediation. In this final chapter we take a step back, place HIT in the overall context and attempt to shed light on the way forward.

In order to revitalise Japan's stagnant economy, a critically important issue is how to raise successful microenterprises, small and medium-sized enterprises (SMEs), and emerging enterprises or businesses. Lending to small business, however, commands high credit examination costs relative to income from loans, which prevents small-business lending from becoming a general activity of financial institutions.

In 2004, the Incubator Bank of Japan, Limited, was established as a bank specialising in SMEs lending and general term deposit taking. The operations of the bank, however, became the subject of an administrative disposition of the Financial Services Agency and its president was arrested on charges of hindering a criminal investigation. On the other hand, there is Fast Retailing, the operator of the Uniqlo apparel chain, which in a cooperative arrangement with Grameen Bank, which started making loans to impoverished people, has been attempting to resolve poverty, hygiene, and education, among other issues, through the manufacture and marketing of its apparel.

These example cases demonstrate the essential difficulty in effectuating small-scale lending. Grameen Bank's success in establishing a track record owes much to

S. Shiozawa (✉)
Faculty of Economics, Keio University, Tokyo, Japan
e-mail: shiozawa@econ.keio.ac.jp

N. Yoshino and S. Kaji (eds.), *Hometown Investment Trust Funds: A Stable Way to Supply Risk Capital*, DOI 10.1007/978-4-431-54309-1_6, © Springer Japan 2013

the fact that borrowers are known to the bank, that is, the bank holds sufficient amounts of information to obviate in large part the need for credit examinations from scratch. Lenders in Japan, by contrast, used to have almost no information on borrowers from the ranks of SMEs and emerging companies. Except for some financial institutions with ties to their local communities, such as regional banks, credit unions, and credit cooperatives, lenders in Japan are facing substantial obstacles in establishing small-scale lending as a business. Nevertheless, raising successful microenterprises, SMEs, and emerging companies is indispensable for revitalising Japan's stagnant economy.

Hometown Investment Trust funds (small investments aimed at regional development) relate to measures centred on suitably inclined individuals to help stimulate local economies by supporting the funding of businesses, traditional industries, or entrepreneurs, provided there is potential demand for their products. The aim is to provide appropriate information, enable individuals to find transparent investee counterparties, enlarge the pool of growth capital funded out of individual financial assets, identify potential demand in communities, and stimulate local economies.

Hometown Investment Trust funds can be looked at as local community infrastructure for information-sharing that functions for market participants as public goods or as club goods which are shared and consumed by a limited circle of participants (Shiozawa 2012).

2 The Background of HIT Funds

As considered in the first and second chapters, the overview of the flow of funds in Japan and other countries in Asia presents a financial structure centred on ordinary banks.

Due to the Basel capital adequacy requirements, banks are unable to provide sufficient amounts of risk money. Moreover, given that deposits are subject to principal guarantees and are posted for definite periods, banks' approach to investing term deposit funds has by necessity been conservative. For Japan's real estate investment market, however, the hope has been that it might serve the function of providing stable investment opportunities for the public's personal financial assets by linking real estate markets and financial markets. But, currently the volume is only about 33 trillion yen, which is not large enough. In particular, fund inflows have been in steep decline since 2008, which demonstrates the limits to hopes that regional financial institutions might cover the inactivity of Japan's large banks and foreign financial institutions.

About 60% of personal financial assets in Japan are cash and deposits, with a very small amount of holdings in securities such as securities and bonds. To a degree, this situation reflects risk avoidance of individuals. It is also true, however, that it would involve outsized transaction costs for individuals to locate appropriate investment vehicles, leaving direct investment in individual businesses an unrealistic investment proposition.

Moreover, depending on the type of business invested in, recovery of the investment might take several years and hence require funds available over the long term.

In many cases, banks are therefore unlikely to lend. At the same time, venture capital is scarce in Asia, including Japan, and cannot be relied on as a source of funds either.

This situation makes it an urgent task to create a framework for small-scale lending as funding for local microenterprises, SMEs, or business operations.

3 Characteristics of Lending to Microenterprises, SMEs, and Emerging Companies and the Significance of HIT Funds

In contrast to lending to large corporations or consumers, the following characteristics apply to lending to households, microenterprises, SMEs, and emerging companies.

(1) Diversity
Significant qualitative differences segregate the business operations of microenterprises, SMEs, and emerging companies. Especially with respect to emerging companies, judging the technical aspects of individual operations or products involves complexity that requires the right kind of expert knowledge for credit assessments, a requirement that raises the cost of the credit assessment. Since the business earnings of borrowers are in large part dispersed over future periods, the formation of estimates poses difficulty. Since many such businesses are also unable to post collateral, loans assume high-risk characteristics.

(2) Difficulty of information collection
Many microenterprises and SMEs have insufficient financial statements, among other business data, and the credibility of those that do exist might present issues. Consequently, any kind of statistical treatment based on such data is highly problematic. Businesses are increasingly operated by high-aged business owners, often commingling personal and business affairs in their operations, with problems attached also to their willingness and capability to provide information disclosure. Although some financial institutions do aggregate data such as default ratios and recovery ratios, etc., the methods used in such calculation are not without issues. Additionally, methodologies must be established for their practical application and also the aggregation of sufficient data volumes is necessary. From a cost perspective, it is therefore highly inefficient for individual financial institutions to perform all of these preparations on their own, making some form of database sharing desirable.

(3) Small scale
Since the businesses concerned are small-scale, generally so are the loan amounts. To be sure, the same is true also of consumers and households. If combined with the diversity referred to above and the difficulties in aggregating information, however, the sum of attributes marks the most striking characteristic in finance for microenterprises, SMEs, and emerging companies. It shows that compared with the wholesale lending to large corporations or pools of households, generally the proportion of the cost of the credit assessment relative to the loan amount is outsized in the case of lending to microenterprises, SMEs,

and emerging companies. Based on these characteristics, it can be said that the cost of the credit assessment and examinations for loans to microenterprises, SMEs, and emerging companies is relatively high whilst lending income is relatively low. Consequently, when transactions take the form of loans from banks to individual businesses, under the current system it would generally be difficult to operate in the profit zone.

Lending to microenterprises, SMEs, and emerging companies or individual businesses would prove consistent with the varied latent needs of individuals. However, implementing such lending would require on the part of the borrowers the disclosure of full information and on the side of the lenders a correct perception of the risks involved and the willingness to act at each lender's own responsibility. In these regards, the current situation is quite inadequate, with a host of issues left that need addressing. Specifically, markets must be created capable of effectuating financial transactions meeting the requirements of both borrowers and lenders. At the same time, mechanisms must be designed that provide incentives for the voluntary information disclosure by microenterprises, SMEs, and emerging companies as by other borrowers.

Currently, various types of programs exist in Japan for the support of microenterprises, SMEs, and emerging companies. First, there are statutory measures. Second, there is funding support through government-related financial institutions. This funding support from government-related financial institutions is supplementary to private sector financial services, but in substance its significance has been changing from the quantitative supplementation type of old to qualitative supplementation. The qualitative supplementation of funding support comes in the shape of taking risks that private sector financial services are unable to incur. From the perspective of managing private sector assets, however, doing so is in conflict with the basic stance of government-related financial institutions, which are obligated to prioritise safety.

Third, there are management support and technical support, which include, among other things, the Small Business Innovation Research (SBIR) based on the Act for Facilitating the Creation of New Business as well as business incubators run by local public bodies using government funding as facilities for helping raise R&D type businesses.

Lastly, as public goods or club goods, there is the creation of communal infrastructure mainly for the purpose of information aggregation. The significance of this communal infrastructure resides for investors in facilitating the provision of selection criteria and for microenterprises, SMEs, and emerging companies in the avoidance of adverse selection. In other words, in situations where information is incomplete and asymmetrical, the bias of the credit assessment tends to be inverse to business quality. For good-quality businesses, the result is relatively more onerous terms and conditions with adverse selection that reduces incentives to remain in that market. Conversely, a low-quality business is more likely to be overrated, with large incentives to remain in the industry. Moreover, for financial institutions the significance of this communal infrastructure resides in the reduced cost of the credit assessment, in the sense that it facilitates business growth. In this way, the hometown investment system can also be understood as having the qualities of a public good or club good.

The creation of this kind of communal infrastructure and the resulting higher allocation of loan funds to microenterprises, SMEs, and emerging companies, helps promote the reform of industrial structures. Microenterprises, SMEs, and emerging companies, along with maintaining their traditional industries, are also afforded the capability to respond to entirely new areas of demand from the public. If those new areas grow and attract transfers of resources and labour, increases in social welfare will result equal to or exceeding the growth in GDP.

4 Hometown Investment Trust Fund Frameworks and the Current Status

The basic scheme of HIT funds rests on small-lot investments under silent partnership agreements which are concluded directly between the investing individuals and the business operators. HIT funds are positioned to create a new channel for the circulation of funds outside the domains of indirect finance and market finance.

As opposed to investment as part of an average invested in multiple businesses and operations, HIT funds mean individual, hand-crafted investments in investees who are known to the investors. Historically, it has been impracticable for individual investors to obtain adequate levels of information on their investees. Thanks to technological advances today, however, it is possible to connect investors' assets with investees' operations.

Hometown Investment Trust funds have the following special characteristics.

They rest on the willingness of the individual and are not driven alone by a simple pursuit of profit. Individuals have risk tolerances that differ from those of financial institutions. Thus, HIT funds are small-lot financial instruments that do not pass through the balance sheets of financial institutions. Investments can be made also toward individual operations.

Investments made through the silent partnership format pay respect to the independence of management of the investee. Moreover, this format facilitates investment by persons such as civil servants, who are barred from engaging in other activities concurrent with their employment.

Since the investee is known to the investor, it is highly probable that the investor will develop an active liking of the products of the investee's business. For the investee this makes the option conceivable of using in-kind payment for the investor's investment income.

Organizing the fund involves the tasks of intermediation in executing the conclusion of the silent partnership agreement and intermediation regarding investment principal and dividends. Furthermore, an Internet based system for executing investment agreements and for monitoring the operations funded with the investments of the silent partnership is to be established, among other things.

As introduced in Chap. 3, investor attributes will centre on persons aged in their 30s and 40s, about twice as many men as women, which is thought to be close to the percentages of Internet user strata. Moreover, since investment requires a degree of financial freedom, many investors are expected to be aged in their 30s and 40s.

Mentioned in Chap. 4 was an Asian case example where investments of ¥30,000 apiece are solicited in Japan and directly invested in SME micro-finance institutions in Vietnam and Cambodia. Much of the driving motive is the shared notion of an arrangement that combines poverty amelioration and business, with efforts to lower investment costs made through the cooperation with NPOs and other partners.

5 Issues and Outlook

Specific examples of two areas where high hopes attach to the activities of the HIT scheme are considered in Chap. 5, namely the revitalisation of local industries in the course of the reconstruction after the Great East Japan Earthquake and, by way of market development through marketing launched at the local level, the Kokushu (Sake and Shochu) Project. Investment in real estate including business operations and plant facilities is a part of it.

As mentioned in Chap. 2, one of the initiatives under way to enliven regional economies is the Project for Promoting the Supply of Non-recourse Loans Useful for Regional Urban Development. This initiative involves deliberations on creating environments in which regional financial institutions figure as providers of non-recourse loans.

As a novel concept, the topic of revenue bonds has been raised, where under full local government guarantees the new issuance of earnings-linked bonds by a public company or SPC would be permitted, in a way of probing for the right division of functions between the government sector and private sector. Moreover, in connection with the division of functions, Private Finance Initiative (PFI) systems are being reconsidered. Taking a separate approach to the development stage and the stage after business stabilisation, considerations envision banks to lend during the former stage and insurance companies and pension funds to invest during the latter.

Whilst the hope is that HIT funds will see further initiatives and developments in these wider frameworks, many issues remain in order to achieve this vision.

One issue concerns the question of how to disseminate basic, accurate information. Public recognition of the device as a financial instrument needs to be raised and products made distinguishable from fraudulent imitations.

From the perspective of the protection of individual investors, the need arises for the standardization and planning of methods for information disclosure so as to facilitate risk assessment. With a view to enhancing the convenience of the scheme for individual investors, redemption gains and losses should be put together with other financial instruments where aggregate calculation of gains and losses is possible, and appropriate sales commission fees must be set, such as dividend-linked charges.

In addition, it would be desirable to improve the scheme's utility for businesses and promote the participation of blue-chip grade new business operators. Through checks on ethical conduct implemented in the form of a self-regulating organization and through suitable supervision by administrative agencies unethical business operators should be removed and relationships of trust created with investors.

The function expected of HIT funds is to make latent demand visible and help create the supply to meet it. The main factor behind the current stagnation of the Japanese economy is depressed effective demand. Overcoming this situation depends on finding a way to stimulate especially personal consumption. Although for many goods demand is sated, in many other areas latent demand is bound to exist. This demand will not simply present itself automatically and without effort, however. Entrepreneurs are needed who discover this demand, in other words, persons who create additional wealth. Environments need to be shaped to enable these people to become active and in this they must be supported by all areas of society. Naturally, there will be risks and many cases will end in losses. Necessary above all is that information as accurate as possible is communicated and shared.

This kind of system has the properties and fulfills the role of a certain type of public good, a role that cannot sufficiently be met by individuals and private sector business. It takes public support and supply. This provides the basis on which individual investors can identify promising business operators and invest at their own responsibility. Depending on the case, in-kind dividends are conceivable. In this day and age of diversifying value priorities, preferences, and lifestyles, there is bound to be a sea of demand for products that are distinctive and particular. Historically, markets for these kinds of goods needed to have a certain size in order to be successful. Thanks to the advances in information and communication technologies including the Internet, business environments now render also small-scale markets viable. Also in this sense, frameworks like HIT funds, based on technological advances and the rise in the number of Internet users, will likely continue to grow in importance. Whilst many issues still need to be addressed, HIT funds can be an effective mechanism that holds enormous potential for revitalising the Japanese economy.

Reference

Shiozawa S (2012) Philanthropy, NPO, public sector and social benefit. Nonprofit Rev 12(1)

List of Contributors

Editors

Naoyuki Yoshino is a professor of economics at Keio University. In 1979 he obtained his Ph.D. from The Johns Hopkins University; his thesis supervisor was Sir Alan Walters, Baroness Margaret Thatcher's economic advisor. Dr. Yoshino has been a visiting scholar at MIT and a visiting professor at various universities including New South Wales University (Australia), Fondation nationale des sciences politiques (Paris), and Gothenburg University (Sweden). He was an assistant professor at the State University of New York at Buffalo before he joined Keio University in 1991 as a professor of economics. His professional career includes membership on many government committees. Since 2004, he has been a director of the Institute of Financial Research at Japan's Financial Services Agency (FSA). In recognition of his wide-ranging scholarship and contribution to policy formulation, he was conferred an honorary doctorate by Gothenburg University in 2004. Dr. Yoshino was appointed as board chair of the Financial Planning Standard Board (FPSB, USA). He serves as chairperson of the JGB (Japanese Government Bond) Investors' meeting at the Ministry of Finance and as president of the Financial Council at the FSA (Japanese Government). He is a Policy Board member of the Federal Deposit Insurance Corporation of Japan and serves as chairperson of the banks' stock acquisition organization. He was selected for inclusion in *Who's Who in the World* in 2009, 2010, and 2011. Dr. Yoshino received the World Top 100 Educators' Award in 2009 at Cambridge U.K.

Sahoko Kaji received her B.A. degree in economics in 1982 and her M.A. in economics in 1984, both from Keio University, and a Ph.D. in economics in 1992 from The Johns Hopkins University. At Keio, Dr. Kaji has been professor of economics since 1999 and, in addition, programme co-ordinator of the Professional Career Programme (PCP) (http://web.econ.keio.ac.jp/lecture/pcp/) since 2007 at the faculty of economics at Keio. She is also a member of the Council on Customs, Tariff, Foreign Exchange and other Transactions at the Ministry of Finance, and deputy director of the EUSI (EU Studies Institute). Her publications include "Successful

N. Yoshino and S. Kaji (eds.), *Hometown Investment Trust Funds: A Stable Way to Supply Risk Capital*, DOI 10.1007/978-4-431-54309-1, © Springer Japan 2013

Structural Reforms after EMU", *Journal of the Japanese and International Economies* 12, 1998, pp. 507–534; "What Can Countries Do to Avoid a Financial Crisis?", *The World Economy*, Vol. 24, No. 4, April 2000, pp. 567–589; "Economie: la décennie perdue", *Politique étrangère*, Janvier–Mars 2002, pp.67–90; *Kokusai Tsuka Taisei no Keizaigaku* (The Economics of Exchange Rate Regimes), Nihon Keizai Shimbun Publishing, 2004; "What Greece Teaches Us about Democracy", *Journal of Political Science and Sociology*, V. 14/pp. 1–16, 2011/03; *Euro Kiki de Nihon wa Dounarunoka* (What the Euro Crisis Means to Japan), Nihon Keizai Shimbun Publishing, 2012. Further information can be found at http://k-ris.keio.ac.jp/Profiles/0030/0005959/prof_e.html.

Authors

Atsuo Akai is a senior advisor at Morgan Stanley MUFG Securities Co., Ltd. He is a visiting professor at Waseda University, where he is responsible for policy research as a senior researcher at the Center for International Real Estate Research, and teaches in the Graduate School of Finance, Accounting and Law, with a specific focus on securitized products and fixed income investment. Mr. Akai is active in a number of government working groups/panels and industry organizations in Japan. He is an expert member of the National Land Council, in which capacity he is serving as a key member of the committees on several property-related policy/regulatory issues. Most recently he was appointed as a vice chair of the Committee on Real Estate Market Strategy at the Ministry of Land, Infrastructure, Transportation and Tourism. In addition, he was a chair of the JSDA (Japan Securities Dealers Association)'s Working Group on "information disclosure and best practice for structured credit products distribution". Outside Japan, Mr. Akai has been appointed as a chairman of the Global Advisory Council (GAC) of CREFC (CRE Finance Council) and in 2008 was elected to the Board of Governors of CREFC, the first Japanese to be chosen, after serving as a founding co-chair of its Japanese chapter and an editorial board member of CMBS World. He has written a number of books and articles for the investment community in Japan. These include *Global Portfolio and Risk Management* (Kinyu Zaisei, 1998), *Handbook of Global Fixed Income Investment* (Kinyu Zaisei, 2003), and *Finance for City Development* (Gyosei, 2005). Atsuo Akai received a B.S. degree from Keio University in 1987.

Masami Komatsu is the president of Music Securities, Inc. He was born in 1975, and completed his MBA at the Graduate School of Finance, Accounting and Law, Waseda University. He started Music Securities, Inc. with a capital of 500,000 yen in 2000. Its main business was creating a music fund in which fans could invest to support artists. In 2006 he began establishing funds for restaurants and a sake storehouse. Currently, 166 funds in 20 industries and organizations, including forest preservation, apparel companies, professional soccer teams, and furniture making, are in operation under Mr. Komatsu's direction.

Norifumi Sugimoto has been the general manager of the Regional Planning Department of the Development Bank of Japan Inc. since June 2012. He is responsible for policymaking for reconstruction support to the Tohoku District of Japan hit by the earthquake and tsunami on March 11, 2011. His ongoing efforts include the city rebuilding scheme in Ishinomaki, Miyagi Prefecture, one of the most severely damaged areas. Previously, Mr. Sugimoto was the deputy general manager of the Business Planning and Coordination Department and of the Tohoku Revival Reinforcement Office located in the Tohoku branch of the Development Bank of Japan, proactively working on the reconstruction of Tohoku. Earlier, he was responsible for the bank's public relations activities as the director general of the Office for Public Relations and Corporate Social Responsibility. Mr. Sugimoto joined the bank in 1988. While serving the bank, he was appointed special adviser to the Minister of State for National Policy at the Cabinet Office of Japan in September 2011. Prior to joining the Cabinet Office, he was the director for policy planning of the National Policy Unit of the Cabinet Secretariat beginning in October 2009. Mr. Sugimoto received a bachelor's degree in economics from the University of Tokyo in 1988. He was a visiting fellow of the Program on U.S.–Japan Relations, Harvard University, from June 2000 to March 2001.

Yuka Morita works at the securitization department of Music Securities Inc. Her responsibilities include due diligence, setting up, monitoring, and investor relations for microfinance funds. Before her current job, she established the first smoothie store in Imo State, Nigeria, with the aim of bringing in a new business idea from outside the country, creating jobs, and generating income for low-income populations in the local community. The reason she chose smoothies was not only that the smoothie was a new product there, but it also was healthy and could utilize local agricultural products. Ms. Morita earned her B.A. in economics at the University of California, Los Angeles in 2008.

Shuhei Shiozawa is a professor of economics at Keio University. He earned his B.A. in economics at Keio University in 1978, his M.A. in economics at Keio University in 1980, and his Ph.D. in economics at the University of Minnesota in 1986. His main research fields are financial theory and theoretical approach to NPOs and corporate social responsibility. Dr. Shiozawa also worked for the Cabinet Office of the Japanese government as a counsellor for international economic affairs from 2001 to 2003. He is the chair of the committee for promoting the Hometown Investment Fund Trust at the Cabinet Office.

Index

N. Yoshino and S. Kaji (eds.), *Hometown Investment Trust Funds: A Stable Way to Supply Risk Capital*, DOI 10.1007/978-4-431-54309-1, © Springer Japan 2013

MIX
Papier aus verantwortungsvollen Quellen
Paper from responsible sources
FSC® C105338

If you have any concerns about our products,
you can contact us on
ProductSafety@springernature.com

In case Publisher is established outside the EU,
the EU authorized representative is:
Springer Nature Customer Service Center GmbH
Europaplatz 3, 69115 Heidelberg, Germany

Printed by Libri Plureos GmbH
in Hamburg, Germany